— *for* —

LOVE *and* MONEY

VOLUME ONE

www.landforloveandmoney.com
www.reidlancerosenthal.com

Publisher's Note:
This is a work of narrative non-fiction. Except where specifically named, places, businesses allusion to persons and incidents are from the author's recall and perception—actual names withheld at request, or to protect the privacy of individuals, entities, groups or locational jurisdictions. Any resemblance to any other places, people or events is purely coincidental. Any trademarks mentioned herein are not authorized by the trademark owners and do not in any way mean the work is sponsored by or associated with the trademark owners. Any trademarks used are specifically in a descriptive capacity.

Book cover and interior design: Dan Forrest-Bank, FB Edit–Design
Editing: Page Lambert and Tami St. Germain
Cover photo credits—
top: Main rainbow photograph © Reid Lance Rosenthal
middle left: Vermont Farm Panoramic © Robertplotz | Dreamstime.com
middle right: Mountain landscape with horse © Dmitry Pichugin | Dreamstime.com
bottom photo strip *(left to right)*—Yellow New England House © Dwight Smith | Dreamstime.com; rural landscape © Joshua Rainey | Dreamstime.com; Mountain lake © Reid Lance Rosenthal; family walking down ranch road © Page Lambert

ISBN: 978-0-9821576-5-7
Library of Congress Control Number: 2012908774

LAND

for

LOVE *and* MONEY

VOLUME ONE

True stories,
expert advice—
farm, ranch,
recreational,
residential—
large and small.
Told from the
ground up.

Reid Lance Rosenthal

Cheyenne, Wyoming

ACKNOWLEDGMENTS AND SPECIAL MENTION

To all those who have taught me of land, love and money over the years.

To the brave men and women of our military—who sacrifice on many levels to defend our freedoms, including one of the most basic—the right to own, enjoy and profit from the land.

SPECIAL THANKS TO:

Jordan Katie Allhands—Art, web and organization
Jani Flinn—Rockin' SR Publishing
Laura Kennedy—Coordination, media and administration
Deborah "Web Deb" Kunzie—Web design and programming
Devani Alderson—Social media
Tami St. Germain—Copy editing
Dan Forrest-Bank, FB Edit–Design—Graphic design and cover
Tom Dever—Narrow Gate Book Publishing
The great folks at Midpoint Trade Books

To my parents who, among many gifts, exposed me from birth to wide open spaces, entrepreneurial attitude and the land—its power, energy and comfort to the soul.

To my literary editor, Page Lambert, who cajoles, commends and scolds at just the right times, and who continues to teach me just how much I do not know about the wonderful craft of prose.

To my daughter, Jordan, without whose technical skills this book would not be a reality.

And, to America, the opportunity she offers
to succeed, fail and try again—
her values, history, people and the mystical energy and magical empowerment that flow from her lands.

Table of Contents

SECTION III

SECTION IV

This Isn't the City—What the Neighbors Say When You Leave the Room / 157

SECTION V

Conservation— Getting Paid to Do the Right Thing / 191

Conclusion

SECTION I

Finding Land— Purchasing or Walking Away

Chapter One
Does the Land Speak to You?

All land has energy. It will reach out and touch you, speak to you if you open yourself to its power. Land developed with homes has yet another dimension of personality. The concept of energy flowing from the land holds true, no matter the size, region or locale. Some readers will nod and smile at this concept, while others will wrinkle their brows.

What is this energy? The current that flows from a piece of the earth to the soul and senses is metaphysical—part mental, part physical, part spiritual. For some, the sensations come more quickly or strongly, but I am convinced that all people have the innate capability to feel the mystical tug of land.

The key here is to open yourself and remove the shrouds of city and society that block your intuitive radar. You will recognize, with a thrilling certainty, a peculiar and then familiar vibration that emanates from your center and grows stronger, a magnet for the countless waves of sight, smell and sound that combine to form perception.

*****

The attentive land acquirer needs to step out of the societal fabric of modern life that surrounds us, and touch, sense and observe the macro environment, the community, the adjoining parcels and, of course, the property itself. As corny as it sounds, close your eyes, breathe deeply, exhale slowly and feel it. Allow every sense to drink in the audio, visual and olfactory flow that emanates from each and every piece of property. Listen to the pleasant excited tickle in your gut, or the lack of it.

First, write down what you want in your relationship with the land, what you need, what factors are absolute. This will create efficiency, and will likely result in the most satisfactory purchase. Too few people take the time to sit down and reduce to paper their "must haves" versus their "can't stands" when it comes to acquisition of residential land, ranch, farm, recreation or rural acreage or even a home. Far fewer understand the connection with the energy of the land, which may occur with the very first property or not until the twentieth. Rest assured, these rules and the energy of land hold true universally. Firm goals, desired property attributes and financial parameters are key to the successful search for property, a fulfillment of the quest for heart and hearth.

* * * * *

On a hot, dry day in late August 1987, I pulled my three-quarter-ton Ford pickup to rest at the curb in an old-time Montana town. The clicking drone of cicadas hung in the shimmer of high-country heat. I studied the aging real estate office where I was to meet the listing broker to take a look-see at an up-valley, 998-acre riverfront spread for clients of mine. I had always loved this southwestern part of Montana, with its waters still pristine and undiscovered. The jagged peaks of range upon range tugged on the endless blue sky. The hills cradled a wide, fertile and sleepy valley. I liked the energy of this little town: the way the main street curved, unlike the straight shot of most small towns; the eclectic assortment of buildings; and the slow pace of people as they sauntered along sidewalks, taking time to greet and gossip. I was "that cowboy from Colorado"—an outsider. At that time, no outsider had ever purchased a ranch in that valley.

I walked purposefully to the front door of the real estate office and swung it open. Before me were some desks with piles of paper here and there. An older cowboy-rancher type with a slight potbelly reclined, arms crossed behind his head, in one corner. A cheerful middle-aged woman occupied the front desk. She greeted me warmly, but warily. The older gentleman merely sat in the back of the office studying me. This was the listing broker. He was likely comparing my jeans, denim shirt and beat-up cowboy hat with the price of the ranch we had made an appointment to see. He was no doubt wondering if this would be a waste of his time.

He finally stood up, moved slowly toward me and extended his hand. The handshake was firm and sincere.

"Jerry," he offered simply.

"Reid," I returned.

I felt a connection to him and vice versa, though his was grudging. He seemed surprised that our energies were compatible. He pulled out a few maps and hand-traced the boundaries of the ranch across the contours of the quads. He told me a few selected tidbits, not wanting to let loose too much information before he got my full measure. He suggested that we hop in his truck. I grinned at the thoughts going on behind his set and steady brown eyes. I acquiesced.

We sped down the highway, south from town. We passed an array of large and small ranches, most of which were still flood-irrigated. Only a few venerable pioneers had begun to deliver their water through wheel lines. We came to another tiny town, turned off and followed a winding road toward a point where two mountain ranges met and formed a notch. I liked the approach. End of the road. The mountains close, with inviting contours, even on the valley floor. Dense riparian areas with healthy stands of red and golden willow and hardy alder followed the serpentine course of the river. The streambed was set back from the road. I caught an occasional glimpse of enticing riffles. We again turned off, this time on a dirt road.

He gestured at a fence post. "Here is the northeast corner. It corners up there, and up there and out on that ridge, generally speaking." He pointed and leaned out the window of the truck.

The land was a perfect variety of topography, irrigated, with good upper grasslands, stunning snowcapped backdrop, end-of-the-road privacy and ,of course, the river. As the pickup raised dust down the dirt road leading to the main entry, I noticed that there was lots of room for improvement on the place. It could use irrigation delivery, ponds, livestock-related management changes and fence replacement. There was ample opportunity to add value with good land planning and some hard work. There was also a veritable treasure trove of recreational pleasures to be enjoyed. I had done my homework on this area. With sixth-sense knowledge, I knew that the destiny of this valley—with or without my clients—was other than the closed, drowsy community it was on that day. The thought filled me with remorse, and I vowed to do all I could to preserve it, regardless of the surety of exponentially increasing recreational pressures.

I glanced over at Jerry sitting next to me. I really liked him and his steady", quiet discourse. In his world, things didn't change. He hadn't seen the explosion in ranch and recreational properties in Colorado, the beginning of the tidal waves of city folks and coastal dwellers who were destined to engulf the Rockies.

He drove slowly through the front gate. The older-model pickup creaked as it bumped across the cattle guard. Lush green meadows and a dense stand of cottonwoods highlighted the river, the main artery of the ranch. The soft folds of the foothills of the Rubies and the Gravelies tumbled down to the bottom lands. They talked to me, called to me.

I turned to Jerry and said, "I have seen enough for now."

The pickup ground to a halt as he turned his head quizzically. A smile formed on his face. I felt his thoughts: *I knew this young buck couldn't buy this place. Thank God, I haven't wasted more than an hour.*

I grinned at him. "Let's go back to your office and write up a contract."

Dismay flashed across his face. "But don't you want to see the rest of the ranch? It takes half a day!"

I shook my head. The overpowering energy I felt from the place had propelled my decision. I replied, "After the contract is written and submitted, I'll come in and take my time on an inspection. We'll make it a contingency."

Jerry looked incredulous. "What am I going to tell the owner? That you want to buy it, but don't want to see it?"

"Nope, tell him I want to look over every square foot for my clients, and want to meet him, but no sense spending lots of everyone's time until we all know we can make a deal."

The Ruby River Canyon Ranch in Alder, Montana, was purchased by my clients. The ranch was improved over the course of ten years with the addition of mechanized irrigation delivery, one hundred sixty acres of new crop production, riparian protection fences, cross-fencing for holistic grazing, a pond, streambed and stream bank improvements, spring developments, headquarters cleanup and a host of other significant improvements. The ownership group enjoyed the property for a decade and a half, and was delighted with the tax benefits of the grants of conservation easements preserving portions of the resource. Additional properties adjacent to the ranch were purchased. A few portions of the ranch having little agricultural value and not really connected to the whole generated 1031 like-kind exchange funds, which deferred taxes and allowed the acquisition of a larger ranch on another river just miles away. (A 1031 deferred exchange allows a seller to defer tax liabilities on gains of sales of property if strict criteria for investment of the sale proceeds into another "like-kind" property are met within a specific time period.) The larger ranch also was improved and eventually protected by conservation easements. The sales of those two properties spawned further investment for the group. Today, with their money back times ten, they are owners/operators of over five thousand acres of incredibly beautiful ranch lands in Wyoming.

* * * * *

Flash forward eight years, this time in Colorado. As I had done countless times before, I pulled my Ford truck up to a real estate office in the small but typical, reborn Colorado town of Eagle, now bustling with an eclectic mixture of displaced persons from both coasts, city dwellers in retreat from Denver and a smidgeon of the old-time crowd that had dominated twenty years before. There was a feel to this town, too. Definitely western, but with much more yuppie energy. All the buildings had been transformed into the New West, each façade an attempt to recreate the modernized feel of the wild times gone by. A coffee shop bustled with patrons. The vehicles were mostly brand-new or late-model expensive SUVs, rather than pickups, and the real estate office was a swank stone-faced building perfectly organized into cubicles. Smiling, attractive receptionists graced a long curved front desk and waiting area. Not good, not bad, just was.

I grinned as I remembered the dusty, musty, one-room realty offices in sleepy towns with the old-timer ranch brokers in Wyoming, Montana and the still more remote corners of Colorado.

I waited ten minutes, sipping coffee and watching the activity in the reception area. A young woman strode toward me in pressed jeans and a leather belt with a large turquoise buckle, in the latest attempt at western fashion. She greeted me with a wide smile and looked me up and down.

"It's a pleasure," she said with a flutter of blue eyes. "The ranch we are going to look at today is really one of our exceptional listings. It has everything. And great potential for subdivision, also."

I knew the comment was a probe. I said nothing other than, "Howdy."

Her eyes scanned my torn jeans, two-day-old road-travel stubble and sweat-stained cowboy hat.

"I have heard of you," she ventured. "You're involved with quite a few ranches, aren't you?"

"A few, here and there."

"Let's grab a latte, and then we'll go out to the ranch," she suggested and briskly headed out the front door, my cue to follow.

We walked out to her brand-new, loaded-to-the-hilt Ford

Expedition. She saw my pickup covered with the dust of a thousand miles of dirt roads and asked, "Is that yours?"

I nodded at her grimace. On the drive out to the ranch, sipping my triple mocha, I did my own probing. Though my questions were specific to the ranch we were about to see, I ascertained her knowledge of water rights, agricultural practices and wildlife and fisheries populations, and found out she worked primarily on residential listings. She was a competent realtor, but she certainly was not a ranch or land broker.

We drove through acres of subdivisions with newly built trophy homes, most of whose architectural styles were completely out of place with either the old or contemporary West. Many perched selfishly close to neighbors and intruded upon their resources. Others sat on the very tops of hills, visible for miles.

"How often do these folks see their places? What do they do with them?"

"Some people come out for a few weeks a year. Others for a month in the winter and summer." She pointed at a monstrous multi-million-dollar home obnoxiously sprawled on the knob of a foothill. "That one belongs to Mr. 'X,' the chairman of 'ABC' company. I don't think he has been here since it was built."

I grew quiet and took in the approach. The ranch we were going to see was about six thousand acres. That was a good-sized spread, even in those days in Colorado, and far more difficult to find now. We turned off the main road up a narrow canyon past the occasional big ranch obviously owned by persons other than the original ranch family. Here and there were scattered pockets of subdivision with an eclectic mixture of mostly newer structures. A number of land parcels sported new survey stakes. More subdivisions coming.

The canyon was narrow, and I noted that most of the property lay on the north face, a problem in winter at an altitude of seven thousand five hundred feet. Snow took a long time to melt at this high altitude, access would be dicey and snow removal expensive. The creek we crossed at the entry rushed down a steep gradient, so the current tumbled and gushed over rocks. Very difficult to fish and little or no holding water. Casting would be a nightmare and the fish small. We drove into the front entrance of the ranch, which resembled more of a southeast horse farm than a western ranch. Several ponds, distinctly man-made, were placed for ease and convenience, with no attempt to blend with the land contours. The road was a straight shot, perpendicular to the slope. This meant inevitable erosion and maintenance. Most of the hillsides were steep, unusable for livestock, and the north exposure meant limited winter browse for deer and elk.

Although the listing had stated differently, the property did not back to any state or federal lands, a prerequisite in my land searches. The ranch simply did not talk to me. The energy was that of something out of place, not in sync. Very few worthwhile resource improvements could be made. I turned to the realtor, who gripped the steering wheel with white knuckles on the bumpy entry road.

"I've seen enough. I appreciate the tour."

She pulled the vehicle to a stop and looked at me with dismay. "But we haven't seen everything," she protested.

I smiled softly. "Yes, we have. It's pretty enough, but it doesn't speak to me."

Her expression was one of incomprehension. We turned around and went back to her office. We exchanged the perfunctory business cards, and I left.

She did not understand that the energy of a piece of land was as tangible and important to me as the physical properties of that piece of earth. If the energy didn't flow from the land to me, it wasn't the right piece of land. This was the universal truth that guided me. Firm goals, desired property attributes and financial parameters, were key to the successful search. But it was the energy that fulfilled the quest for heart and hearth.

Chapter Two
Grab the Brass Ring: Time to Purchase

You have completed the search for that special ranch, recreational or rural property. Now the real work begins. My long career has involved thousands of property transactions, improvements, acquisitions and sales. I have learned three important things. First, each property, each buyer, each seller and each deal is unique. Second, local markets, local politics (in some cases, state politics), the prospective neighbors and various aspects of the property combine different ingredients to make a one-of-a-kind stew. Third, the recipe must include a professional team and your personal time dedicated to property research prior to ownership, the combination of which will enhance potential success and decrease post-closing risk. Many factors must be taken into account. Assemble a competent local team to assist you and list the team members. Prepare, plan, consider all the details, request disclosure, investigate and research fully. Neglect any up-front steps, and you could end up with a dish of disaster.

*****

It was 2003. A tiny black-and-white ad, stuck in the classified grid at the back of a local newspaper in Wyoming, jumped out at me: "Twenty-eight-hundred acres of pristine mountain land, creeks, secluded, just an hour from Douglas."

I was looking for a suitable 1031 exchange property (see Section III, Chapter 15) to defer a large capital gain on a pending sale of a ranch in Montana. Owned by long-time partners for more than a decade, the Montana ranch had been enhanced pursuant to a ten-year improvement plan. My firm had been the ranch manager, and I took an ownership position in the group in 1999. Values had increased exponentially. Truly an exceptional agricultural and recreational ranch property, portions of it had been preserved by conservation easements and a myriad of significant agricultural and resource improvements had been made since its purchase in the late 1980s. One of our favorite places, we were sorry to let it go, but all things have their time. My partners instructed me to find a property of equal or better value and beauty. I had a tough job ahead of me.

My search parameters concentrated on certain areas, which, due to macroeconomic circumstances, demographic trends and conformance to our acquisition checklist (see *Green for Green* workbook), demonstrated superior agricultural and recreational potential, along with realistic possibilities for increase in value via market trends, agricultural and resource improvements and preservation.

It was no accident that I searched the obscure pages of a small-town paper of southeastern Wyoming, home to the little-known but exceptionally beautiful Laramie Mountain Range. This undiscovered area lies just three hours north of Denver and the teeming Front Range of Colorado. I was sure that this location was "going to happen."

As soon as I saw the ad, I picked up the phone and called the broker immediately. Affable and knowledgeable, he was definitely anxious to make a deal. He persistently pressed for a date to show me the ranch. Although I tried to radiate nonchalance, I anticipated the opportunity with eagerness.

A week later, one of my partners and I met with the broker and the current owner of the property. The seller, a terrific guy, acted very friendly, but he was also cagey and sophisticated. He had purchased the property in a foreclosure two decades prior to our meeting. Even with his reasonable sales price, he stood to make a handsome gain. I gleaned that family issues motivated the sale. The remote property had been on the market for some time, and it had obviously not enjoyed the high-gloss marketing that larger real estate firms were affording their listings in the days prior to the internet taking off. The broker and his seller had apparently been friends a long time.

We toured the spectacular ranch that day by foot and ATV. We saw five different drainages, including a major creek that meandered through miles of the land. Wonderful historic structures begged for restorative attention and preservation. The spread had senior territorial water rights for over one hundred sixty acres of irrigated land. Game trails, browse lines and giant rub marks indicated superb deer and elk populations. The larger creek teemed with trout. The other drainages consisted of small perennial and seasonal creeks and large springs that promised significant pond and upland water development potential. Better irrigation techniques meant room for significant improvements in the hay crop. The ranch didn't talk to me—it shouted. My partner heard the voice too.

Chapter Three
Looking Under the Rocks

Later that night, he and I met and decided to make a run at the property. We took out my contract checklist. Knowing something about the seller's wishes, we decided to ask for seller financing. We discussed other important contract terms that tied into our long-term goals for the property, which were to enhance, hold, enjoy, operate it as a working ranch, preserve it and add value.

Next we discussed the assembly of a long-term team to assist in this and other transactions in a region with which we had little familiarity. The next day we began to negotiate the contract. I spent hours on the phone canvassing my network as well as our few local contacts. We needed to find a reputable surveyor, an excellent real estate attorney, a competent title company and a water rights specialist.

The property was located in the North Platte drainage, which in water rights lingo is considered a "closed basin." The North Platte River and the Colorado River are likely the most litigated waters in the United States. Whether "neighbor vs. neighbor" or "state against state," litigation over more than a century has complicated the seniority, use and diversion of water rights. We could not proceed without knowledgeable consultation with a local water expert.

The final critical component of our team would be a local rancher with a good history in the Laramie Mountains to advise us on growing seasons, crops, local politics, water commissioners, neighbor history and viewpoints, and nearby cattle operations as potential markets for pasture and hay.

Within days, I narrowed the selection to two surveyors, three possible legal counsels, one particular water rights guru and one local ranch operator. I researched the attorneys on Martindale-Hubbel (www.martindale.com). I uncovered several larger surveying jobs where each of the survey firms had performed work and talked to the landowners. I dug up the name of a potential rancher/ranch manager through the network and drove slowly by his place. It was neat, organized, cared for and obviously productive. His home and barns were clean and freshly painted. His horses and livestock were in superb condition.

The next two days flew by with work on the contract draft and the cell phone glued to my ear as I drove to Cheyenne, Douglas and Wheatland. I visited the rancher's homestead one evening and had a cup of coffee. The water wizard and I met at a local saloon for a burger. In the early morning before the survey crews left for the field, I stopped by the Cheyenne headquarters of the surveyor who had received the most glowing recommendations and met with him and his son. On that same trip, I sat down with our number-one-pick attorney, who also had offices in Cheyenne.

I liked and trusted these people and had respect for their acumen. Our team was assembled, organized and brought up to speed, and only four days had elapsed since the showing.

A protracted contract negotiation ensued. The principals and the attorneys painstakingly negotiated details, along with numerous critical financial elements. Every salient point and major question was passed on to the appropriate team member for input. The contract was executed. Due diligence and research followed. Over the ninety-day due diligence period, the property passed every test and investigation with flying colors. This was a fun part of this particular purchase.

Insuring Your Dream Does Not Become a Nightmare

Little can compare to finding, loving and anticipating the conversion of a dream to reality, only to find out after you receive your deed that a neighbor can cross your new land under an old easement, or that somebody upstream can "make a call" on the water rights and dry up your creek. The discovery that sparkling blue, fish-filled ponds are impossible because the soil is too permeable or that the water right cannot be diverted is not pleasant. If that sounds extreme, consider this: What if an environmental hazard lingers from long ago and was never disclosed? What if that problem precludes financing or insurance, or festers with potential physical danger and tremendous liability? What if an adjacent property owner announces plans for a four-hundred-unit subdivision after your closing? What if the seller retains some rights or even a piece of property you believed was included in your purchase? How about an announcement that eighteen-story metal monster power transmission towers are going to be marching across your land? The fact is you cannot be diligent enough in searching for any possible future problem.

An experienced realtor, a knowledgeable real estate attorney who understands water and finance, a good surveyor and your own CPA are vital core members of such a team. For larger purchases, you need to consider having a land-and-resource consultant, an attorney schooled in mineral rights and other specialists. Even then, be prepared to encounter some surprises. Get your team vested in your vision and excited about the land. They will be invaluable throughout the period of your ownership.

A carefully drafted purchase agreement must clearly set forth all matters that the seller must disclose and that you wish to research and investigate. The "Buy/Sell" or "Purchase and Sale Agreement," as it is commonly referred to, is the first formal step in the process. Certain states or Canadian regions are "contract" jurisdictions. Others are "escrow" locations.

Areas that require escrow transactions also require an attorney to draft the Purchase and Sale Agreement. The Broker prepares only the "Binder," an outline of the contract details.

In contract negotiations, the realtor prepares the contract or oversees contract preparation. Many realtors in contract states or provinces are averse to using attorney-drawn contracts or forms that are different from the standard approved forms of the real estate commissions of the various states and provinces. Many sellers lack the experience to trust an attorney-drawn contract. There is nothing wrong with using a standard real estate form, so long as it is relevant for farm, ranch, vacant or rural ground. However, do not attempt to buy a ranch or rural property using a residential house contract. The printed real estate forms must be as carefully perused as any other document.

The Team

Create and consult your team, but remember that your advisors can only do so much. The team is not the buyer of the property—you are. While the team members may offer great insight and enthusiastic support, never forget that it's your money that is being spent to achieve your dream. In addition to review by the team, read every document yourself. If using a pre-printed format, pay attention to the numerous little boxes that allow the seller or buyer to elect certain rights or confer certain obligations and liabilities (see *Green for Green* workbook).

If you have a buyer's broker with whom you have a Buyer's Agency Agreement, that's great! A qualified broker experienced with land can be your first line of defense. He or she can bring invaluable experience to the purchase equation. Residential realtors typically do not have the specialized knowledge necessary for most land transactions. Remember that the seller's agent or broker owes their allegiance and agency by law to the seller, not to you. If you are not represented by a buyer's broker, or if you decide not to assemble a full acquisition team, I highly recommend that you at least have competent real estate counsel domiciled and licensed within the same state, and preferably the same county as the property you wish to purchase. There is no substitute for local knowledge, network and contacts. Do not sign any purchase agreement without having it reviewed by your attorney and buyer's broker. A seemingly innocuous detail or an inconspicuous term can be the cause of severe post-contract regret.

Don't be afraid to add special provisions or conditions to your contract. Don't be too bashful to ask for something you want, or too lackadaisical to care. Don't blow off an opportunity to get things right at the very outset. Additional provisions or conditions can be suited to your needs and goals, to your financial reality and long-term plan for the property (see Chapter 14). If you employ a standard-form contract, these matters can be set forth in the "Additional

Provisions" section. If the selling broker whines that there is only so much space on the preprinted form, look him or her in the eye and say, "Then let's add some additional provision pages as an addendum or a continuance of the Additional Provisions Section."

The contingencies section of the contract and any additional provisions are your primary contractual shields. These sections allow you to investigate the land, the title and a host of other matters. This affords you and your team a chance to perform the due diligence necessary to avoid wrecks and ensure that the property can actually fulfill your short and long-term goals. It is primarily these clauses that allow you to exit the contract with a full refund of your earnest money if your investigation reveals problems or contingencies that cannot be met.

The basic criteria of a sound purchase agreement includes: price, terms, finance, place and date of closing, conditions, contingencies and additional provisions. However, layered into each of these basic contractual components are a myriad of advantageous or disadvantageous details. Many times it is the details that make or break a deal, ensure long-term success or cement eventual failure.

These details can protect you from unsavory circumstances; for instance, if the seller were to attempt to void your contract and sell the property to someone else, effectively leaving you high and dry, or refuse to return your earnest money. These details can also protect you if the property does not check out based on your due diligence research. A well-written agreement allows you to "reach back" after closing, if a problem should later arise from a lack of disclosure by the seller or seller's agent.

The agreement should also address any additional matters over and above those which applicable state or provincial statutes state clearly do not merge with (terminate), but survive, a closing, such as a seller's continuing post-closing warranties or promises. It is the details that may afford you closing or financing flexibility if external economic, governmental, terror-related or similar matters of force majeure occur prior to closing. These general examples are only a few of the many possible scenarios that should be on your radar screen. (An outline of contract considerations developed by me and used by my firms over four decades are in the *Green for Green* workbook.)

The contract must provide adequate time for investigation of local and adjacent properties and conditions, as well as property-specific matters. Environmental considerations, either existing or which might potentially arise in the future, water rights and resources, soil and geologic conditions, particularly where one plans to grow or build, mineral ownerships, leases and rights, title matters and vegetative disease infestations if the property is forested, are all among other important matters to research (see Chapter 4).

The Property Title: Pay Attention!

Matters of title are critical. Many, though not all, of the countless possible "clouds" that can hover over land title issues are listed in the *Green for Green* workbook, along with a sample Title Insurance Commitment. A few examples include: Who owns the underlying mineral rights? Are these leased? To whom? Is there access, utility or other easements, or reservations for certain types of uses by others? Do the sellers own the entire property or just a portion? Do they have the full legal authority to sign your deed? Is there a break in the chain of title over the years or centuries? In other words, could some owner prior to your seller assert a claim? I highly recommend experienced legal review of the title conditions and the documents that evidence those exceptions.

The Contract process is a curious mixture of challenges, short- and long-term thought, satisfaction and, at times, frustration. Patience, an even temper, team coordination and comprehension of seller motivations are all keys to finally getting an agreement inked. If the seller becomes intractable on truly key issues, or something in your gut warns you, then walk away.

Otherwise, remember the moment the land called to you, smile, enjoy this fascinating process and get it done. If you feel your energy waning under the weight of lifting these "due diligence" rocks, take a deep breath and reconnect with the magnetic pull of the land that inspired you in the first place. Let the energy of the land refuel you and remind you of your dream.

Chapter Four
Buying Smart: The "PPPPP Rule"

Not everyone, of course, is looking for six-thousand-acre ranches. Many prospective buyers are searching for one-, five-, twenty- or one-hundred-acre parcels to use as getaways, vacation homes, a tangible safety deposit box for their dollars or for eventual retirement. Perhaps they are self-employed and now have the opportunity to move out of the urban, suburban or exurban living areas and run their businesses from a more remote and enjoyable location. In some cases, the current malaise of the overall economy has spurred them to accelerate their goals. Still others are looking for a good investment, with an eye toward eventual disposition or change in land use. Size, price and location are not the sole criteria to the sanctity of the procedures employed, observations made, questions propounded and research undertaken. It is the combination of want, need, heart, brain, knowledge, feel and science that play a part in a final decision to purchase rural property.

Too many people jump on the internet with a dream notion and a vision of an area and a property lodged ephemerally and non-specifically in their head. This is bound to lead to disappointment and frustration. Failure to employ "PPPPP" (prior planning prevents poor performance) will result in a waste of time, energy and money for the acquirer and their agent. In the worst case, a purchase can devolve into a bad deal.

Step-by-Step Deductive and Empirical Forethought Is a Must in Looking for that Special Place

First, write down the absolutely key components of your dream parcel, the things that you must have. Live water? Pond development potential? Fishery? Wildlife? Agriculture? A place for horses? Approximate size? Can the land be part of a subdivision, or does it need to stand on its own? Must it back to federal, state or conservation lands? What type of neighborhood do you prefer–eclectic, old-timer, newbie, new West, remote? What amenities do you require in the nearest town? Simply milk and bread, butter and eggs? Or more? Do you have horses or other livestock? Do you want to be able to pasture year-round, or are you willing to buy hay? Do you want to grow hay? Must the property already be improved with a home, or are you willing to build, or remodel an existing structure to suit your personal style and tastes? What is your budget? What proximity do you desire to metro areas, airports, skiing, recreation and bodies of water?

A property already improved with a decent residence—although there are limitations and guidelines discussed elsewhere in this book—will generally afford the opportunity to finance 60 to 85% of all or a portion of the purchase on a fixed long-term mortgage. In some cases, the seller may carry some paper, usually short-term but with relatively beneficial terms, via a note, mortgage, deed of trust or what is called a contract for deed.

Raw land is more difficult to bank finance, particularly in slower real estate markets. This is currently exacerbated by federal and state bank examiners feeling that, generally, land is high risk. They go out of their way to "classify"—that is, downgrade—bank assets that consist of land loans. This restricts the bank's capital and ability to lend to anyone for anything (see Chapter 12). Count on 50% as the maximum you'll be able to borrow, and you will need very good credit to do so. Be honest with yourself. Once you understand what financing you are comfortable with and can qualify for, the difference between the price you are willing to pay and what can be financed is the amount of cash you need. It serves no purpose to spend time looking for and falling in love with a property, putting it under contract, investing the emotional and financial effort and then in the end finding out that you simply can't afford it.[1]

The purchase of land, whether rural, recreational, farm or ranch property, is a distinctly individual matter. Although I have been involved in all types of properties, the land that appeals to me personally is wild, remote, improvable, at the end of the road and backs to wilderness. This may not be your preference at all. You may be more comfortable with white panel fences and ten acres surrounded by similar properties, within fifteen minutes of the mall. There is no good or bad, no right or wrong. This is about personality, lifestyle, needs, wants, must-haves and can't-stands, all encompassed in a longer-term plan.

The FIVE Great Rules of Real Estate

Some may know they want to be in the Carolinas along the coast, or somewhere high up in the Rockies near skiing or with horses, or in the mountains of California within striking distance of the teeming metropolitan areas, but with some peace and solitude on the fringe of more densely settled areas. Even those who don't have a specific geographic location in mind need to realize that the rules are the same.

[1]A detailed checklist for property searches and a worksheet for determining general financing capabilities will be found in the *Green for Green CD/DVD* workbook.

When purchasing real estate, pay attention to these five rules:

1) Never trust your neighbor's taste. Particularly on smaller properties, you may find the perfect place, only to be saddled with neighbors whose idea of great land use is a jacked-up truck without wheels and hot pink paint. You want to avoid the anguish of having someone else's taste ruin your dream.

2) Never purchase a property without seeing it or having the absolute right to see it before your earnest money goes hard (becomes non-refundable), or your contract becomes irrevocable.

3) The government can and will change the playing field. Keep your nose to the wind for trends in property rights, tax and environmental and other policies (see Section III).

4) Always have an exit strategy and options, even if you believe this is the place you are going to buy and never sell. Lives and lifestyles change unexpectedly. Micro- and macroeconomic events affect the best-laid intentions and carefully made plans. The long-term plan with attention to exit strategies must be integrated with your search and acquisition. While a plan is distinctly personal, there are some requisite elements for your safety net. These include: Is the property sub-dividable? Can you shave off a chunk of the land to sell if you need money in the future, without affecting the value of the rest? Who is your target market, if you ever need to unload that new home or remodel? What has been the average number of days on the market (DOM) for similar properties over the last ten year

period, including at least one up and one down real estate cycle? How quickly can you get out of a deal if Chicken Little arrives and the sky is falling?

5) Prior planning prevents poor performance or, the "PPPPP" Rule.

Keep in mind that the purchase of the property is just the beginning. There is ongoing home maintenance, taxes, insurance, fencing, landscape maintenance and perhaps agriculture; as well as the inevitable list to improve the property or buildings. These are all expenses, and some can be rather spendy. Include these items in your budget. Buying a property that talks to you when you lack the funds to fully create your dream can be frustrating and lessen your enjoyment.

Do you have an estate plan? If you get hit by a rolling hay wagon, what happens to the property and its equity? The *Green for Green* workbook contains a checklist to stimulate long-term planning. Do not be bashful or dishonest with yourself in setting forth clear and concise, short, medium and long-term goals for your land. This will begin to drive your property plan, management strategy and ongoing operational budget, as well as assist you in formulation of must-haves/can't-stands, acquisition criteria and eventually, heighten your enjoyment of your purchase.

Most of all, open yourself to the possibilities. Feel the energy of the land. Savor it. Let it speak to you—listen. If there is anything not quite right with the energy, trust your gut. The old adage applies: "Know when to hold 'em, know when to fold 'em, know when to walk away and know when to run." Energy not just right?—Don't spend another minute! Energy feels just fine, but the facts don't check out?—Regretfully, but resolutely, walk away. Energy fine and the mechanics are sound?—Don't hesitate, buy it!

Chapter Five
Partners Are People: There Are Good, Bad and Very Bad

Buyers are often tempted to "go partners" purchasing a piece of land, or any type of real estate. Your partner may be your parents, or your children. A partner may be a friend, or a spouse. These types of partnerships are known as Joint Ventures or General Partnerships. Often in these types of arrangements there is no Partnership Agreement. Not a good idea! In less frequent instances, there may be more than two partners, or many "partners" in the form of a Limited Partnership (LP), Limited Liability Company (LLC) or Sub S Corporation (S-Corp), which might include people you barely know, or don't know as well as family or friends.

A "partner" in a S-Corp is a "shareholder," a "member" if in a LLC and a "Limited Partner" if their interest is via a LP. In *all* these types of entities profits, losses and tax flow to each individual partner, not to the entity. Each structure has its own peculiarities. There are slightly different tax treatments, varying rights of partners and powers of managers in the case of LLC companies, or general partners and officers in LPs or S-Corp, respectively.

Regardless of the structure you choose, certain steps must be followed for these entities to be "legal." Articles of Organization for an LLC, Articles of Incorporation for a S-Corp and Partnership Registration via various forms must be filed with the state government.

Certificates of Authority are necessary if your entity is formed in one state, but doing business in another. Some local governments require further registration. Always consult a *local* attorney. A tax ID—commonly referred to as a "TIN" (Tax Identification Number) must be obtained.

The above is a synopsis of creating your business entity. The paperwork is mostly forms. However, the agreements which govern the rights, responsibilities, powers, liabilities and authorities of the various parties—while required to have some "boiler plate" language—are the key to the operation of the entity, and its assets, distribution of profits or other benefits in happy times, or resolving disputes if things go wrong. Do not underestimate people's propensity to be nasty if your best laid plans fall apart, or to be greedy if your deal is a smashing success! These documents are known as "By Laws" if for a S-Corp, and a "Limited Partnership Agreement" if for an LP. An "Operating Agreement" governs the workings of LLCs.

The folks who run the show are the officers and directors in a S-Corp, the managers in an LLC and the General Partner (many times a corporate entity) of an LP. In a GP—unless the Partnership Agreements provides differently, the partners have equal say.

A Buffet of Choices

Remember the "PPPPP" rule! How well you think and plan in advance at the inception of your entity may well determine the success—both of the heart and the wallet—of your venture.

When the sun is shining, the birds are chirping and the money is flowing partners generally have wide smiles. Even then however, a partner can go AWOL, cause angst and for ulterior personal motive allege some type of impropriety or complain about their share of proceeds, even though it was agreed upon up front. This type of adversarial and self-centered behavior will occur far more frequently when the sky is stormy and things are not going well.

While many partners will stand shoulder to shoulder with you in tough times, there will be, almost guaranteed, partners who become completely self-interested, cause uproar and, in some cases, jeopardize the interests of other partners and the land. I've seen and been involved in situations where partners refused to sign sales documents even though the property was being sold at a profit in tough economic times. Other partners contrive excuses to not pay their share of ongoing expenses or debt service when partnership funds run low. Marriages and family relationships can go south for reasons having nothing to do with land, the real estate or the partnership. Life happens.

I have found it highly beneficial to sit down prior to becoming involved in any of these types of entities and make a list of what can go wrong. As imaginative as you may be, the list is never 100%. Your own personal situation, the personal situations of other partners, macroeconomic events, government related interference or change in the playing field, taxation, interest-rates, market demand and costs associated with production if your land is a farm or ranch or produces other goods are but a few potential ugly circumstances. Your own incapacity, or death, even the cost of fuel, i.e., national energy policy, can affect use, transport of commodities or willingness to travel in the case of remote lands and properties. Your advisors can help you with dark ideas you haven't thought of. If experienced, your realtor, attorney and accountant have all seen deals go bad and have witnessed partners go off the deep end.

Once you've developed your list of what could go wrong

possibilities, you're in a better position to put together contingency plans to handle these aberrations in the conduct of the business, of the entity, and the management and operation of your land. Equally as important, you will have a feel for what you need to build into your partnership, and LLC agreements or corporate bylaws. What will happen if the entity runs out of money and checks must be written to pay interest to the bank so the property is not lost? How should a situation in which some partners contribute and others do not be handled? What happens if a true micro or macro emergency occurs and your land or property must be dumped in an extreme exit situation? Who has the power to make day-to-day decisions? Who can sign checks or commit the entity to contracts, legal actions and other facts of business life? What happens, if for any reason partners just don't get along? Limited partners in a LP, members in an LLC and shareholder in a S-Corp, unless the documents provide otherwise—or they sign notes or other security instruments—generally have limited liability under the laws of any state. How far do you want this limited liability to extend? If you are running the show as the manager, president or general partner do you need an indemnity from the partnership or the partners if things go wrong and you get in a jam acting on their behalf?

There's an interesting mechanism, which is both fair and absolute that can be employed if the abrasion between partners in a deal is irreconcilable, dangerous to the respective partners or the partnership and is undermining the entity and the real estate. This is called a "Shotgun Buy-Sell". Its ironic simplicity is stunning, and in my experiences, it works.

In a Shotgun, two or more partners who are at odds each have an opportunity to buy the other out. Either can make an offer to the other for all or portion of their partnership interest. The amount of the offer is determined by the offering partner. Here's the beautiful twist. The partner to whom the offer is being made can either accept the offer, or can buy out the offering partner's interest for the same amount! In other words if partner Joe want to buy out partner Sally and offered her $10 for her partnership interest, partner Sally has only two choices—accept the $10 and transfer her interest to Joe, or elect to buy Joe's interest for $10. Obviously, this keeps folks honest, eliminates arguments and provides resolution. Don't be surprised, however, in really bitter situations if a partner to whom the offer is being made simply refuses to abide by that provision of the partnership agreement and you have to go to court to enforce the Shotgun, or other provisions of the agreement.

Don't Trip Over the Up Front Rules

If you are partnering with other than family, the government could consider a partner's purchase of the interest in the entity a "security." Strict rules govern the sale of securities if the transaction is to be exempt from the very stringent requirements of a public or quasi-public offering, and the attendant nightmare of paperwork and expense.

Good legal advice and an accountant who knows the vagaries of tax and other financial treatments are highly recommended especially when choosing a form of ownership that involves a partner(s). Why? There must be full disclosure, financial projections, a subscription agreement (with partners agreeing, among other covenants, that they are not acquiring their interest with intent to sell it) and that they meet minimum "sophisticated investor" financial requirements (including a minimum net worth of $1 million exclusive of their personal residence). Because we live in a time of increasing regulatory control, rising taxes, local, state and federal governments hungry for money to fuel past programs, ongoing services and—unfortunately, in many instances—unchecked expansion, outside forces will undoubtedly affect your land and the lives and other investments of your partners. In perilous economic times, folks get into trouble. They can have short memories when it comes to agreements to chip in money, contribute their share of work, be available, make timely or critical decisions—or sign on the dotted line with the bank or other lender when it comes time to extend, renegotiate financing or approve a sale.

Many Partners—Trust Your Nose

Virtually all of us have heard horror stories of a married or unmarried couple, or friends, where things go wrong on a personal level, and one spouse or partner skips out leaving the remaining partner alone with the cost, expense and liability on land, farm or single-family residential housing. Obviously, this often results in a struggle to carry the debts, many times resulting in material adverse credit and financial consequences. That situation is not limited to personal relationship-based partnerships. It happens in arms-length transactions between partners in small and large real estate deals everywhere, all the time, and with increasing frequency in today's economic climate. Refer to the "PPPPP" rule. It is not the end all/be all shield against financial, mental and emotional stress when there's a breakdown of any type in a partnership or ownership of real estate, but proper preparation can afford you legal rights, and a structure to partially protect yourself, or take the adversarial steps you must to make a partner live up to their responsibilities, or divest them of their interest and authority.

Long ago, back in the 70s when things were rocking and rolling in residential and multifamily real estate (prior to the four-year tenure of Jimmy Carter), I was approached by a man slightly older than me whom we shall call BM.

BM had optioned a well located, twenty-six-acre parcel that nestled just off the interchange of a major arterial and Interstate 25, in a booming area just north of Denver. Multifamily units and apartments were a hot ticket, and enjoyed all sorts of tax benefits. The land met our criteria for that type of intended use—it laid out beautifully over rolling hills, had great access and exposure, full utilities, the end product was perfectly suited for that micro market and the view of Denver's skyline was terrific.

I had doubts about BM from the first time he shook my hand. He didn't look me in the eye as he told me about this "great piece of property" that he had just optioned, wanted to build two hundred apartment units on, and was now offering to joint venture with my construction company.

For those of you about to skip forward because twenty-six acres of land on the fringe of an urban area, planned for a two hundred-unit apartment complex, "doesn't apply to your situation," hold your horses. This, and the other stories in this section, contain universal truths about real estate, partnerships, money, short memories and how the acts and lack of acts of others can cause untold financial and emotional strain, if you are not properly prepared.

We liked the land, the due diligence checked out, the market was perfect and I convinced myself that with the right joint venture agreement, including stiff protections and safeguards learned from previous partnership type deals, we could protect ourselves if my gut instincts about BM proved to be true.

A lengthy joint venture agreement was drawn, with extensive protections, particularly for our side of the venture. We maintained virtually all control. BM had some say in the design of the units and like matters. BM had to sign the dotted line for the bank right alongside us, even though it was our financial capacity that provided most of the foundation for the financing.

The units were designed, development work began on the land, financing was obtained, and the project was underway. I noticed on several occasions during the planning process that BM would pretend to be unable to approve this or that in the design scheme. A few weeks would always elapse while he supposedly "intensely pondered" what he really wanted. This caused delays and ran the interest meter, but he would always come back with an approval, providing he received some type of additional "bone," which usually involved money, percentage or interest. He was obviously wheedling the deal.

Two years into the Carter presidency the project was completed, our management company achieved a quick lease-up and we were pleased with the end result. Carter's concept of high taxation (70% top rate), expanding government and printing money to fuel the expansion, was beginning to have its inevitable effect. Unemployment rose, inflation crept rapidly upwards, fuel prices exploded, interest rates rose and demand fell.

The note on the property was a floating-rate note. We were protected with a ceiling (top possible rate), and the bank was protected with a floor (lowest possible rate). We foolishly agreed to a ceiling higher than the project could support without an increase in rents thinking (also foolishly) that interest rates could never get that high. Wrong. Macro events far beyond your control, (as discussed in Sections II and III of this first volume of *Land for Love and Money*) can and will reach out and grab you. You will have little, if any control.

Interest rates quickly rose to stratospheric levels, and the project could not generate income sufficient enough to pay the debt. The loan had been structured as an intermediate term (three-year) acquisition/development/construction loan, which would roll over into a long-term permanent mortgage. If checks had to be written for any reason, the joint venture agreement called for BM to put in money equal to his smaller percentage, along with our much larger share of the expense pie.

BM conjured up a plethora of excuses, accusations and complaints about how the apartments had been built—though he had approved every step of the planning and construction process, management of the joint venture, management of the apartments and more. Using these excuses he refused to write his share of checks, though he had eagerly grabbed his earlier share of proceeds. He also refused to sign on the dotted line for the rollover of the intermediate term loan to a long-term mortgage (on which I had negotiated a significantly lower interest rate than what we were paying on the shorter-term, floating-rate financing).

The situation became tense. Threats of legal action flew back and forth, though from our vantage I knew nothing could be gained and the real estate would suffer.

I finally called BM one day and said, in essence, "If this continues we will lose the property and no one will have anything. What's it going to take to get this resolved?"

BM's reply was what I expected. "I don't care if we lose the property. I have been paid my fees, the economic outlook is bleak, I am not collectible and it will be years before there's a profit. Since I have minimal assets, the only signature that means anything down at the bank is yours, so in reality you have all the risk."

Shortly thereafter, though he had no legal or equitable basis for the request, BM agreed to take $25,000 to relinquish his entire right, title and interest to the real estate, and be removed from the joint venture. In context, that $25,000 would be roughly $125,000 in today's dollars. The money was paid, BM was removed (though not without further foot dragging and additional attempts at extortion) and ultimately the project was saved and sold at a profit. However, the gain was much smaller than it would have been due to the time and expense involved in the dispute with BM, the deteriorating economic conditions and the delay in getting the high interest rate, intermediate loan converted to a lower rate, long-term loan. Not to mention brain damage and diversion of time and energy.

The Inescapable Truths

There are five universal land and real estate morals to this story.

1) If you have a gut feeling about someone and it's less than perfect, heed your instincts.

2) If a potential partner has exhibited any propensity to delay, leverage, use subterfuge to gain advantage (tangible or intangible), particularly if the delay or impediment is detrimental to that partner also, this person is absolutely going to be what I call an "extortion partner." They will not change. Run, don't walk from the deal.

3) Never do business—or fight—with someone who has nothing to lose.

4) There *will* be macro-economic events, including government policy, taxation and market conditions which *will* affect your land and real estate—and your partners. Try to plan for the worst case.

5) The most carefully drawn partnership, Limited Liability Company, joint venture or other type of agreement that creates a multi-person interest in land and real estate, or that entails shared responsibility, means nothing unless the person on the other side of the paper intends to follow the agreement.

Many Partners—Potentially Many Problems

Flash forward to current times, and a beautiful, eight-thousand-acre ranch property in a western state. The land has water, mountains, agriculture, fisheries, big game and excellent grazing, and took many years to put together. The property occupies an exceptional location with exceptional resource attributes and the appraised (and real market value) is far higher than the debt. Various ranches were assembled to create this beauty using a combination of structures, including a LP, a LLC and a pre-existing "C Corporation"[1], which the seller of the property foolishly formed when it was in vogue in the 1950s.

The LP had owned other ranch properties since the late 1980s. There were seventeen partners in the LP. At that time, I had no interest. Rather, my ranch management and consulting firm acted as advisor and consultant to the owners, supervised their due diligence, advised them (along with their counsel and CPA) on business aspects

[1]A corporate entity in which profits are trapped (i.e., do not flow through to the shareholders [partners]) and which pays tax at the maximum rate at the entity level, such profits taxed and then again when distributed as a dividend to the shareholders.

of acquisitions, planning, formation of the LP and other structures. We managed all of their various ranches. I knew each and every one of the partners individually. There were some that I liked more than others, but all seemed to be standup, financially capable folks who shared common interests, primarily the preservation of wild and agricultural lands, hunting and fishing.

From the late 1980s up until 2008 things went very well for this group. At their invite, I purchased an interest in their Limited Partnership and became President of the General Partner in 1999. It was a shoulder to shoulder deal. Everybody had skin in the game, i.e., investment. The other person with management authority (an attorney) and I guaranteed the financing of property and property acquisitions. The partnership documents allowed the general partner to ask for money if it was needed, but no Limited Partner was obligated to loan money to the LP unless they wished to. However, the partnership agreement allowed for dilution—the increase in ownership for partners writing checks and the decrease in interest for those who did not.

Things progressed nicely. The partners were happy, the LP was profitable overall, fishing was good, there was little discussion and certainly no dissension at the annual partnership meetings. Many of the partners became good friends with one another. Then came the economic meltdown of 2008.

Also at that time, one partner ran into medical issues. Another had purchased a business that began to flounder. A third suffered a death in the family with various estate problems. A fourth, also for estate purposes, including the looming re-enactment of the 55% death tax after expiration of the Bush tax cuts, split his interest out 25% to each of his four children. Many of the partners, some just retired, and many approaching retirement age saw their retirement accounts materially adversely impacted in the economic wreck. Many saw income from other investments reduced and values plummet. Some had extraordinary expenses such as weddings, or college for their children.

Difficulties were engendered by generally deteriorating economic conditions, personal situations of a number of partners, a slowdown in demand for several years for any type of real estate, anti-wealth policies of both the Federal—and on this ranch—the State government and problems the smaller bank which had financed the ranch was having on a number of loans that had nothing to do with this group or this land. These unforeseen nasties were exponentially exacerbated by the macro whammy of expanding government (much the same as Jimmy Carter's but on steroids) and a rapidly expanding regulatory environment in the brave new world of Dodd–Frank Wall Street Reform and Consumer Protection Act (Dodd–Frank).

All this unexpected macro "fun" attendant to the financial meltdown, and the Great Recession, materialized after the initial financing had been done. Then the deal was "blessed" with Dodd–Frank. Though all other terms of loans had been complied with, and the loans provided for extensions and longer-term financing in 2006 when the ranch was finally fully assembled, the new regulations and soft market adversely affected other loans in the lender's portfolio, and tied the bank's hands. To prevent its loans from being classified (see Section III) they had to take the position that the loan would be renewed only if there was a 10% annual principal reduction ($250,000 per year) in addition to semi-annual prepaid interest.

Several partners pulled a "BM" and refused to write checks. Other partners stepped in and loaned monies over their *pro rata.*

The bank acquiesced to a cessation of the unanticipated principal pay downs (after approximately $500,000 had been paid), and lowered the interest rate to market from several percentage points over market. Because the various LLC and LP documents were properly drawn, the final result for those partners who stepped up to the plate will be a much larger percentage of any gains from the sale of the ranch. Those partners who drummed up excuses to not pay, will suffer the opposite consequence. Had these worst case mechanisms not been put in place up front more than twenty years ago, the contributing partners would have had no incentive to do so, and the ranch most probably would have been lost, along with everyone's investment.

SECTION II

Things Not Thought of—The Fiscal and the Politics

Chapter Six
State/Local Politics, Finance and Taxes

I am astonished at how many people call or contact me, their hearts set on a certain location in a particular state, for various reasons—they visited there in the past and liked it, they heard about it from friends, it's close to family, it holds some special mystique for them based on their life experiences, word-of-mouth or other reasons. Few, if any have ever investigated the fiscal, tax, economic and political trends. It's as if—in their minds—that land simply sits out there on its own, immune to all other influence. The land is not immune.

Remember, land is both a tangible and *long-term* asset. You have heard the stories of one purported real estate guru or the other who bought houses and flipped them for quick profits in days, bought land that tripled overnight and similar tales. These are the rare exception—they are by no means the rule. Real estate is a long-term asset. If you're planning on buying something to turn quickly, perhaps you'll be lucky, but I strongly urge you to have a long-term contingency plan. So far in this volume—and we have barely scratched the surface—you're becoming aware of events, circumstances, personalities, government and gotchas that can slow a deal down or roll it upside down. Some of the other stories later in this first volume of *Land for Love and Money* will make you blink.

You will scarcely believe them, but they are true.

Because land is a fixed, tangible, long-term asset it cannot be moved. If things start to go sour in the community, the county, the state or even the region in which the land is located, you're pretty much stuck. If property taxes double because local government is broke, or schools are under water, too bad for you. In a desperate state, sales tax, personal income tax rates, surcharges, fuel tax and service charges *will* increase. There will be attempts at covert levies upon any increases in the value of your land. Again, you are pretty much stuck. If the state or locality is prone to strict and ever-increasing land use or environmental controls, zoning mutations, an ever-burgeoning bureaucracy and governance of private property rights, the trend is far more likely to accelerate then regress.

Be aware of the *area* in which you are purchasing. In this and upcoming volumes of *Land for Love and Money,* we discuss your gut perceptions of the people in the community. How friendly and helpful they are, or are not. How tolerant of divergent views of "outsiders" they are, or are not. However, in this chapter I'm alerting you to something far more mechanical, and potentially devastating.

If a local, county or state government is broke, running huge annual budget deficits, has been unwilling or unable to change its course of out-of-control spending, this could mean a significant problem for you and your land in the future. In addition to the better publicized annual budget deficits governments run, and whether or not they have a cumulative surplus or negative number on their balance sheet, all governments have unfunded liabilities.

You've heard much of the primary national debt of the United States which, as this book is written, is $16 trillion and climbing. But the unfunded liabilities, Social Security, Medicare, Medicaid, government pensions are estimated—depending upon the expert—at an additional $60–$100 trillion. No, that is not a typo!

The same is true for governments at local and state levels. For instance, California, depending upon who is cooking the books in Sacramento in a particular year, admits to being $16+/- billion underwater on its cumulative balance sheet. It runs an annual deficit of hundreds of millions of dollars—and that number is with fast and loose accounting. The unfunded liabilities of California, however, such as social programs and especially pensions, are estimated to be between $105 billion and $210 billion. That is not a typo, either. This is a state where limited offshore drilling rights, if leased, would result in royalties which would balance the budget and make significant inroads in state debt. The state refuses to take that step. This is a state which is not only curtailing spending, but keeps increasing social programs and entitlements for citizens and noncitizens alike. It is a state that is losing jobs, losing population, losing industry, has increasing income tax rates and sky high and increasing property tax rates, all with the icing of increasing state and local sales taxes.

I'm not picking on California. New York has many of the same problems, as do several other states. Connecticut, for instance, currently has a governor and legislature hell-bent on raising taxes to some of the highest levels in the United States. Illinois, despite the great economic recovery examples of its neighbors in Indiana and Ohio, continues on the same path as California.

Wyoming has no income or corporate tax, and low sales tax. Nevada is the same as are several other states. In some years Alaska actually writes a check to its citizens in amounts which can range from $1-$6,000 depending upon the year and the price of oil, all derived from excess royalty revenues from energy production and transport. Texas has seen significant job growth and a net in-migration of three million folks over the past five years—many of them from California. Florida is another state with no income tax and certain other beneficial, citizen and business friendly structures. Montana has no sales tax, but relatively high personal income tax brackets.

It serves no purpose to do a schedule or chart because these matters are fluid in all states and localities. But the general trends, the corporate culture of the state, can be pretty much relied on for the short, intermediate and (unfortunately for some states), long-term. Some states are more protective of private property rights than others. The Western states have huge quantities of federal and state lands—in some cases comprising 60% or more of the total square miles within state boundaries. This creates other opportunities and pressures, and—as discussed later in this book—dangers.

Current statistics, employment, population trends, new business formations, tax rates, annual budget surplus/deficit, debt and future pension/social program liabilities for various states and localities can easily be found online. Don't just look at "the now," study the trend for the past ten years. It's a fair indicator for the next ten years. Even if states wayward in their fiscal policy completely changed their attitude and operations tomorrow morning, it would take years to see meaningful results. Their tremendous debt overhang, on which interest and principle must eventually be repaid one way or the other, will not vanish. Remember that governments have only one source of revenue. You. And your assets—particularly your land and property because they know, just as you do, that these are fixed assets.

Pay attention to political trends in states and local areas too. While some may think this is a political comment, it is nonetheless true. Liberal or liberal trending governments tend to spend more, have higher debt, higher taxes and believe in more regulation. More conservative governments tend to believe in lower taxation, less regulation and have balance sheets that are in the black, or at least salvageable. Then there are states that are in flux. The front range of Colorado, which comprises most of the state's growing population, has become more liberal. The western part of the state remains conservative. Colorado is now at the point where liberal trends from the East Slope dictate policy for the entire state, sometimes with calamitous results for small communities west of the Denver metropolitan area. The upheaval in Wisconsin is well publicized. New Jersey, Ohio and Indiana having become more conservative, enjoy the opposite trends. Tax rates have been cut, employment is growing, state expenditures are declining, the budget is on its way to being balanced and long-term debt is being tackled.

There is more to your land than just the land. Remember the "PPPPP" rule, and one of the five universal truths (see Chapter 5), your land is not immune—macro events including government policies and taxation *will* affect the financial viability of your land and property, and therefore the amount of joy you derive from your real estate.

Chapter Seven
"Did You Remember the Shovel?"

About fifteen years ago I helped some clients purchase a rural property. The forty acres had a small creek and a great little one-hundred-year-old house. Randy and his wife, Nancy, had some terrific plans to restore the home in historical context and improve the land. It was their first real estate purchase, a huge dream and a big jump from the urban apartments that had always been their home. This was one of my rare engagements as a "realtor." Normally, I use my realty license for deals or transactions for partners, or in conjunction with lands or properties in which I'm personally involved. But I liked this couple, and they were truly novices at land and real estate ownership. I found exactly what they were looking for. The forty acres was the perfect place Their smiles and excitement at the closing table were far better reward than the commission check.

We walked back out to their Ford Explorer after the closing, talking.

"Congratulations. I know you folks will enjoy fixing up that property, developing that little pond you want and making a home for yourselves."

Nancy hugged me, "Oh thank you, Reid. We would not have known where to begin!"

Randy nodded in agreement, stuck out a beefy paw and shook my hand enthusiastically.

It was late afternoon and I asked, "I presume you're headed out to the acreage?" Both heads bobbed up and down.

"We want to get started right away," Randy grinned. "With so many things to do I don't even know where to begin."

"As many things as you do, believe me there will be that many more you'll see to do, and which will need to be completed." I laughed. "What type of equipment have you bought?"

They looked at each other, their eyes wide. "How about tools?" I asked. The two of them exchanged glances.

I chuckled, "I know you're excited to get out to the homestead, but if I was you I'd swing by the hardware store first, pick up a shovel or two, some big toothed metal rakes, a pitchfork, axe, sledge, wedge, and tomorrow, I would look in the *Mini Nickel* and see what's out there in the way of a small used tractor with a loading bucket, and a PTO on the back so you can use it with other attachments as your work gears up. You might want to think about a lawnmower too."

Randy looked embarrassed. "We never thought of that." He cleared his throat, "Where is the hardware store?"

I laughed and shook my head, "Follow me. I'll come down with you and help you get outfitted."

Contractors or Fools—Your Only Two Choices

People who have never purchased land, or a home with land are accustomed to "The Homeowner's Association will do it for you," of condominiums, apartments and urban settings many times don't know to think about basic equipment. Even a third of an acre can require an investment of $500 to $600 in tools. The alternative, of course, is to pay that amount or more every several months to have the work done for you by contractors. Far better to be self-sufficient.

The size of the piece of land that you are purchasing, and the types and nature of any improvements, will dictate the amount, type and power of the equipment you'll need to improve and maintain your asset. Anything over ten acres definitely needs a small tractor—and tractors are sexy! As you get up into the twenty to forty acre range, equipment for fences is a must. A PTO (Power Take-off) unit on the rear of that tractor will allow attachments such as a post pounder or augers. There are even mini backhoes which attach to the rear of the tractor, work off the PTO and are truly handy tools. An assortment of interior and exterior hand tools are also necessities. Hammers, wrenches, screwdrivers, pruning shears, axes, hatchets—the list is long but only needs common sense to compile.

If you have done your homework—"PPPPP"—you'll know your end goals for your property, have them prioritized, scheduled and budgeted. Make sure that budget includes the tools and equipment necessary to accomplish the objective. If you have livestock, the list multiplies exponentially.

There's nothing more frustrating (and this is the voice of experience), than awakening, raring to go, in the coolness of the early morning, the day's project a welcome task you have been looking forward to, only to find that the implements critical to getting it done are on the "forgotten item list." Nothing breaks cadence or delays jobs more than not having the tools, equipment or supplies on hand to complete work.

For places in excess of forty acres, I would give serious consideration to buying a small bobcat. These are some of handiest pieces of machinery ever devised, and most are rigged for every type of specialized attachment you can imagine, and then some. Some type of trailer is a must for hauling supplies from town, moving fence or carting the remnants of remodeling to the dump.

I am frequently asked by clients and partners who are making the jump from city sidewalk to land what equipment I recommend. My answer is always the same: "The smartest landowner, rancher or farmer on the planet is one that owns nothing that can break, and nothing that can die." That always gets a grin.

Don't go overboard on your equipment or tool purchase. Buy only what you need. Used equipment, especially in a smaller rural area—has typically been well maintained. It is the rare instance in a small community that anybody will pass off a piece of junk to you.

In more populated settings inquire as to a reputable dealer. Make sure there's a warranty. If you buy from a private party, have the equipment checked out thoroughly by a qualified mechanic familiar with that brand, make and model.

Buy only what you need. That's the second time I said that! I often see people on a newly acquired acreage literally have to build an adjunct garage or barn to house all the toys they rushed out and purchased. This equipment sits around, barely used, costing unnecessary expense. I am not recommending specific brands or models. These change, particularly with used equipment. Who the owner is, and how the machinery was cared for, is as important as the manufacturer, age and model.

However, I would recommend you stick to known brand names. If your machinery does have to be serviced it will be far easier to find a mechanic—particularly true the more remote you are. The availability of parts is another consideration. You might wait a very long time to get a "wing for the Dodo brand" and, when it comes time to sell equipment, your potential buyers may not be as foolish as you were. Each of the manufacturers has their color. Caterpillar is yellow, John Deere is green and Ford is blue. My recommendation is stick with one of the rainbow. And don't forget the shovel!

Chapter Eight

Give Back to Get Back: Plan for the Land

Land is one of few, and possibly the only asset that affords an owner the opportunity to contribute to the overall environmental good of the planet via restoration, enhancement and preservation, while simultaneously generating not only a deep sense of spiritual satisfaction but also tax savings and gain through the exponential added value of the improvements.

Whether you're buying a third of an acre lot in an exurban setting, a twenty acre horse set up with twenty acres in the hills of California or a ranch of thousands of acres in the Rockies, there's always a way to add value to your land. I've noticed many folks get fixated on the structures and building improvements. These would include the house on that small residential acreage building lot, barn and corrals on the California horse farm or a ranch compound and ancillary structures in the Rocky Mountain example.

Residential acreage is of course a unique class. In those cases, the home is obviously a key asset and generally the largest single component of value. However, under all lies the land. Just like big pieces of the earth, small tract value is dictated by location, area and "amenities." What you do with the land around the structure plays a key role in value. In larger acreages, the improvements to the land—whether they are agricultural, resource, aesthetic or recreational—

become the single largest driver of value. Ironically, lavish structure improvements can thwart sales interest. Folks buying the large multi-million dollar tracts generally can afford to build what they wish. Your idea of a lavish rural home may not coincide with theirs!

Conservation Easements Lower Tax and Death Tax— A Good Thing for the Land, Maybe a Great Thing for Your Family

Because many people think linearly and fixate on the project or improvement at hand, they lose sight of the big picture definition of value. The value to your soul can't be quantified. It is priceless. Financial value is realized primarily through capital gains (long term profit, currently taxed at 15%) at some point in the future, if and when you sell the property. At least in the current tax climate, this is your lowest tax, and therefore your least expensive income and most lucrative form of gross profit. Tracts that are large enough (five acres or more), which have Real Conservation Value and can grant a conservation easement[1], can realize value on the tax side from an ecological donation not only in the immediate tax year, but donations are also likely to lower federal tax in a number of future taxable years via Federal deductions (and in some states, additional tax credits). The big bonus is that a conservation easement also fixes value for inheritance and estate purposes, diminishing the effect of the highest tax rate paid on any transaction under current tax law in the United States.

Some people will raise their arms in the air and shout at me

[1]A conservation easement grant is the donation of certain property rights. In simple terms these rights have value. The appraised value of the rights donated decrease income tax liability. The grant of conservation easements is discussed in Section V. Additional discussion of easements will be covered in great detail with more real-life examples in upcoming volumes of *Land for Love and Money*.

for terming death, "a transaction." It's not. But the events that are triggered after the death of a loved one, a family member or yourself, are all transactions. Under current tax law, those transactions cost you up to 55% of the net value of an inheritance off the top. This tax, which you typically have less than a year to gather, can force you to subdivide your land, sell your land and in the worst cases—particularly in tough economic times—force you to greatly cut price on property to get it sold to pay the tax man—or lose it to the tax man.

Basically, a grant of an easement fixes a value for estate purposes on which the easement is granted based on the *after* easement appraisal. Besides saving big tax dollars, this may allow you to add value through future land and resource improvements that will not be taxed at 55% rate. A grant can afford you the ability to leave a greater net inheritance to your heirs. This can make a sizable difference in their lives, and, although the government hasn't figured it out, tax savings via these mechanisms are beneficial to employment, the economy, GDP, investment, and therefore, in the end, increases rather than decreases revenues to the government.[2] A knowledgeable CPA and attorney should always be consulted when making major decisions of this nature.

Think Ahead—Big Picture!

When you acquire a piece of land, think about what you can do to add value to the property in addition to building, remodeling or rehabbing structures. There are special cases—historical rehabilitations, historical easements and historical façade

[2]Using capital gains rates as an example: when capital gains rates were cut in the early 1980s revenues to the government increased by approximately 28%. In 1993 when capital gains rates rose, revenues to the government decreased by an estimated 21%. In 2003 when capital gains rates were again pared down, revenues to the government again increased 21%. The pattern is irrefutable and is true with virtually any and all individual or business taxes, including the death tax.

easements—which deserve attention because they can add value and reward you with tax savings dividends on many different levels, while also preserving a portion of America's history. These will be discussed, along with real personal experiences, in *Land for Love and Money, Volume Two.* While fortuitous, historical easement opportunities are not common.

Prior to a closing, I sit down and put together a budget spread over time, based on anticipated and realistic cash flows and operations, or money available from partners if in a partnership type deal. I prioritize these potential enhancements on a number of different levels. I give equal weight to adding value to the land and creating operational income. I give secondary value to esthetic effect, and distant tertiary consideration to the "Gee, that would be fun to do" affect. Of course, all is driven by your projections of available cash, and return on an invested dollar of improvement funds.

Let's take, for instance, a one-thousand-acre ranch, Rock Point Ranch, having several miles of the Big Hole River in Montana. This spectacular ranch was owned by a partnership in a venture with others for a number of years in the 1990s and early 2000s. The western boundary of this beautiful piece of property rose to rolling high desert foothills along the horizon, framing the view of the craggy peaks of the Pioneer Mountains. A sizeable portion of the bottom lands were irrigated. The Big Hole River, one of the last undammed rivers in the United States, rushed its wild course in alluring braids for miles alongside the southern boundary of the ranch. It was secluded, but only seven miles from the nearest little town, and thirty miles from the nearest "big city" of over three thousand.

One of the key considerations when making improvements in

land, agricultural or resource, is achieving as many multiple value and operational goals with one improvement as possible. In the case of Rock Point Ranch, improvements which could benefit agriculture, recreation and livestock were painfully obvious. Riparian Area Protection Fences protect wet areas—rivers, springs, creeks, ponds and lakes. This one single improvement[3] allows for pasture division, affording better control of livestock grazing and thus can increase weight gain. It protects fisheries because it stops riparian area overgrazing, which leads to sedimentation, stream bank trampling, sluff and other nasty environmental effects to waterways.

Because these types of fences have very high conservation value, they are often eligible for up to 50% cost-sharing from the United State Department of Agriculture (USDA) through the Wildlife Habitat Incentive Program (WHIP), Environmental Quality Incentives Program (EQIP[4]) and other mechanisms. Because they improve and maintain water and streambed quality, they are a boon to fisheries, increasing the number of fish (population) and the size of fish (biomass per population unit). Additionally, because riparian areas generally include trees, shrubs, aquatic grasses and other flora and fauna, habitat for wildlife and water fowl is increased. More wild critters roaming your land and better hunting for hunting enthusiasts, adds value and is particularly fulfilling for sportsman owners.

So, this relatively simple improvement affects value by enhancing

[3]Fencing types are varied, but four strand wire, intermittent wood and metal posts, runs about $1.75/per lineal foot. Labor charges vary in different parts of the country. With light equipment the fences can be built by the owner.

[4]For detailed information on appraiser designations and changing appraisal requirements, see url links in the Reference section.

wildlife and fisheries and improving agriculture and livestock operations. It simultaneously increases operational revenues because recreation (hunting, fishing, even "vacation" operations) can be converted to operational revenues. At the same time, increases in agricultural revenues via either increased numbers of AU (animal unit—one one-thousand-pound beef cow) or higher weight gain per AU, can be realized. These are key components to income. There are numerous studies that indicate healthy riparian areas increase the amount of water available for irrigation. This benefits crop yield, particularly in more arid areas. Again, you have increased both value and operational income. This is a multiple, many-tiered return of profit, income and value for your invested dollar. You've enhanced the natural qualities of the land, which also generates that deeper, spiritual satisfaction, and your further reward is financial gain.

Water improvements can also result in many different beneficial income and value benefits via a single improvement. A well-planned pond will create or enhance fishery[5], promote and increase overall population of wildlife and waterfowl, can result in better pasture utilization if it is an upland improvement (cows like to hang out near water). A water improvement in a formerly dry upland area will keep livestock in that area and result in better forage utilization, beneficially affecting your entire livestock operation. Obviously, the esthetics of water features are highly coveted by humans.

A well-located pond will enhance late season water storage, can lower insurance costs if accessible to rural fire trucks as a water source and can provide additional source or augmentation for irrigation depending upon your water rights. Again, a single action achieves

[5]Location, design, depth, permitting, cost and a number of other factors must be considered.

many goals. Many times these improvements can generate values in multiples of $5 to $10 for each dollar expended.

Using Rock Point Ranch as our example, we fenced off all the riparian areas, about seven miles of fence, which at that time cost approximately $35,000. Half was paid through a cost share obtained from an EQIP contract from the USDA. After proper permitting we enhanced several existing ponds that were in pathetic condition, and various other water features. Virtually all bolstered the irrigation system. Several enhanced existing fisheries. With the new fencing in place to control livestock, we were able to reseed a number of fields doubling grass yield. We completed other land, resources and agricultural fixes, too. We also did some work in the ranch compound—mostly the visible, such as restoring the exterior of several deteriorated structures—painting, repairing, replacing rundown fencing and revamping the corral system.

It was the sum of the resource, agricultural and land improvements that created additional real value and increased operational income on Rock Point Ranch. The carrying capacity of the ranch increased by almost one hundred AU. Hay production rose by 40%. That stretch of the Big Hole River, along with several miles up and down stream owned by other groups of ours or neighbors of like mind, saw dramatic increases of fishery productivity according to Montana Fish, Wildlife and Parks (MFWP) biological reports. I can say from personal observations that big and small game populations, and migrating waterfowl numbers increased significantly, as did the quality and size of antlered animals.

Our group had purchased Rock Point Ranch in a joint venture with a delightful couple. For a number of reasons they needed to divest themselves of their interest in the ranch and it was agreed that it would be sold. It is noteworthy to mention that we purchased this property with a conservation easement from the Nature Conservancy already in place. There was enough latitude in the easement, and the property was spectacular and unique enough that we went ahead with the purchase; however, it's not how we would have negotiated the easement had we been the original grantors (see Section V).

Despite being encumbered by a less-than-perfect conservation easement, the ranch sold relatively quickly in the early 2000s and there was a gain of approximately $700,000 over and above original purchase cost, cost of carry and the cost of improvements. Our original combined investment, plus improvement costs, was approximately $500,000. That's an approximate 125% cash-on-cash return in six years. Though the venture had planned on keeping this ranch for decades, that age-old reality, "Life happens," happened. Had we not made the value-added improvements to agricultural, ecological and recreational resources, such a gain would have never been realized.

Another ranch, in Wyoming, managed by my firms and owned by another group with which I'm involved, began an ambitious Upland Water Improvements Program when they acquired the property in the early 2000s. Twenty three ponds of one half to several acres each were planned and permitted at spring sources and along small creeks. To date, eleven have been built. All store water for release in the late dry summer and fall months, benefiting the entire basin for miles and miles downstream from the ranch. Two are key to full utilization of valuable Territorial (pre-statehood) Irrigation Rights. All increase livestock carrying capacity. All but one have become viable self-sustaining fisheries. The storage helps to stabilize flow in the main creek that runs through the ranch. The higher, more constant flow has greatly improved that fishery. Migratory and resident elk populations doubled and though we haven't done a formal count, just via visual inspection mule deer populations have likewise expanded. There are now antelope in certain parts of the ranch near these features that were never there before. Build it and they will come. This ranch is being held for the long-term. In fact, this group hopes to hold most of it forever. Therefore there's no sales data to rely on, but the appraisals of portions of the property after these upland water improvements indicate an increase in value of 400% or more within a year of the improvement being completed. That's four dollars of value, plus the boost to operational income, added for every dollar of improvement cost.

Some of you reading this are asking, "What does this have to do with me? I own an acre, or five acres. I can't build eleven ponds or build seven miles of fence." True. But you can undertake the exact same types of improvements on your land regardless of size. All things are relative. If you own a small acreage with a viable water source, research the permit process and construction cost of a water feature, pond or fisheries enhancement project. Literally any piece of property over two acres, or on which you will be running livestock and horses should be properly fenced. In the case of smaller properties the fence can be electric or portable giving you greater latitude. A small acreage agricultural improvement will not be an eight-hundred-acre crested wheat seeding, or a one-hundred-acre alfalfa project, but you can certainly put in a few acres of hay, if you have the space, the water and the growing season. Even our one-third acre residential example can contain one or two large vegetable gardens for your family. If America's current course continues, this could have value greater than simple economics. On the smaller

—less than two acre—land tracts, the major component of value will likely remain the structure, i.e., the house. However, there are many things you can do—most of them gratifying work you can do yourself—to enhance the appearance of your property and capitalize on the aesthetic component of value with landscape, plantings, proper orientation of shade and creative use or construction of deck spaces and outdoor living areas.

None of these things are likely to happen, or if undertaken are likely to be successful, if they are not part of your thought process prior to purchasing the land. One more example of the "PPPPP" rule. Volume Two of *Land for Love and Money* will contain additional stories of monies well spent on all types and sizes of land for successful improvements, monies wasted on bad ideas and the most cost-effective approach in ram rodding all of these types of enhancements. These improvements can both fulfill your heart and fill your wallet.

SECTION III

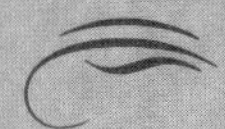

GOVERNMENT, REGULATION, FINANCE, THE PURCHASE, THE SALE— ROWING THROUGH THE PERFECT STORM

Chapter Nine

You Want a Loan? (Banker Slaps His Thigh and Laughs)

Dodd-Frank Act—Diabolical Regulation

In this chapter, I'm going to lay it on the line for you with some fundamental facts about the current regulations, explain sordid situations that cost you money, all guaranteed to drop your jaw and what all this means to you as a potential borrower. Then I'm going to give you some pointers on how you can maneuver successfully in economic conditions where the deck is already stacked against you, and get you ready for the flipside of the coin—the silver lining of great opportunities and terrific imaginative finance options outlined in Chapter 13.

Today's economic, financial and regulatory environment is not conducive to land loans from conventional lenders. In many cases, such financing is impossible to obtain. Cash equity of 30 to 50% is a necessity, as is impeccable credit. Even then there are virtually no banks making land loans. The primary outlets for land loans at the current time is a federal agency known as Farmer Mac (Federal Agriculture Mortgage Corporation), which is in actuality a guarantor of a large percentage of a loan which might be originated through a participating bank, or Farm Credit Services, a land bank with quasi government ties but privately owned and operated. Both outfits prefer production land—farm or ranch that produces income (land that will produce operational income—crops, livestock and ancillary cash flow).

Underwriting criteria for all loans, especially land loans, has tightened considerably. Appraisals are discussed in Chapter 10. Review (second) appraisals are now commonplace in real estate lending and land loans. In addition, the borrower or guarantor must show sufficient ability to pay the interest and principal on the loan. None but the very largest corporations can get land financing without a person, a human being, being liable somewhere in the chain of the loan security, whether as a maker (the person who signs the note) or as a guarantor of a note executed by another party, for instance your farm, land, or property GP, LP, LLC, or S-Corp.

So, unless you have lots of cash, sterling credit, enough personal income to service the loan after all of your other monthly expenses, and the operational cash flow of the property can additionally debt service the loan, you will probably not be getting a land loan from a bank.

Dodd–Frank
Horrible to Begin with, Barreling Toward Horrific

Under Dodd-Frank, there are a myriad of regulations now percolating down from folks who know little to nothing about markets, next to nothing about real estate, and, in some cases have motives other than providing opportunity to citizens and strengthening the economy. Even the few lenders still lending on land require very significant cash equity and very low loan to values ratios. The loan to value ratio, or LTV, is the ratio of the loan amount to equity based on appraisal. If your appraisal is $100, and the loan is $50, you have a 50% LTV.

This situation will worsen before it improves, if it ever does. The knee-jerk reaction to the financial meltdown which spawned

Dodd-Frank punishes the market, buyers and sellers of real estate, and banks (when the problem was caused by government policy to begin with). Though the regulations behind Dodd-Frank are only 20% drafted, there are already calls by Senators, such as Dianne Feinstein (D-Calif.), for more regulation, yet another knee jerk to the just announced $2 billion trading loss by JP Morgan Chase. This insidious degradation of the system has been compounded by political and ideological expediency.

Loans for smaller residential acreages on which you intend to construct your home are possible if you tackle the problem in reverse order. If the land needs to be purchased prior to building (a good idea!) then, first, get a commitment for the permanent mortgage on the home based on your credit, but subject to final plans, specs and appraisal based on its future construction. Next, use that mortgage commitment to obtain a commitment for a construction loan to build the home and pay off the land. Finally, use the construction loan commitment to obtain a short term land loan, which will contain many of the onerous terms referenced earlier in the chapter. You could streamline the process by using the same bank for the land and construction loans. Ridiculous? Preposterous? Yes. But, you ain't heard nothin' yet. Read on.

Unless repealed, the 80% of the regulations yet to be written for Dodd-Frank promise to impose even more stringent guidelines on lending in general, real estate, and in particular, land loans. The regulators believe most land ownership is speculative. This may or may not have to do with sinister policies and attitudes at the national and international level such as the United Nations so-called Agenda 21 (see Chapter 12).

Banks in a Vise You Get Squeezed

It is important to understand generally how banks are monitored, regulated and slapped—or shut down—if they don't follow rules and regulations developed by clueless folks in an out of touch, far away capitol.

Because land is number one on the hit list at the highest levels of government, that corporate culture is filtered down through rules and regulations to the folks in the field. If a bank does not adhere to these rules, it is scrutinized far more closely by government auditors known as Bank Examiners. Bank Examiners visit banks between one and four times a year. A very strong, highly solvent bank (the great majority of its loans performing—i.e., timely paying interest and principle as required) may only get one visit a year. When the examiners visit the bank they go through the loan files. They check to see if the bank is in compliance with all the rules, that all those countless pieces of paper your banker asked you for when you obtained your loan, are in the file in proper form and order. They also check the value of the land, the appraisal, the loan amount, terms, whether or not it's current (performing) and the financial wherewithal of the borrower at that time. Financial statements more than ninety days old now must be renewed. Appraisals must be within the last twelve months for existing loans and within ninety days for new loans.

If the bank is out of compliance on any of these matters, including missing or misplaced documents, the loan file is red tagged and the asset may be "classified". Without getting down in the weeds, there are five basic levels of classification. The first is just "pass," which means they're going to review this file for sure next time they visit the bank, or they have some doubt as to the bank's compliance. The worst is level five, "loss". That's a nonperforming asset on which collection has or is likely to commence. Collection means a lawsuit, foreclosure, or other type of legal action.

There are many other government regulations that affect your purchase of real estate, the Financial Institutions Reform, Recovery and Enforcement Act of 1989 (FIRREA), Department of Housing and Urban Development (HUD) Disclosures, Truth in Lending, the list is endless.[1] I'm not even going to explain what these acronyms mean or we will get sucked into the weeds of tens of thousands of pages of government regulation, most of which do little to protect you, all of which make borrowing, especially on land in the current environment, more time-consuming, costly and far less likely to be approved. Dodd-Frank is the umbrella silliness and exponentially more dangerous and debilitating than the rest of this bureaucratic blizzard.

It is critical as a purchaser or owner of land or real estate that you have a general concept of what is happening behind the scenes at banks of all sizes, particularly small and midsize banks in smaller communities. These "little" banks are the lifeblood of main street, small business, and local real estate. One needs to understand the regulatory nightmare that has been created by a partnership of politicians—many of whom have no experience in land, real estate, or free markets. Some of these politicians really believe that they're protecting the consumer or financial system. Others dislike free-market capitalism, land ownership, and banks. Still others are driven by ideology or ascribe to principles, theory and policy such as Agenda 21—a United Nations edict that is beginning to infiltrate various areas of this country. Mixed together, this cauldron boils a witch's brew of red tape, rules and regulations and hard regulatory hammers

[1]For detail on FIRREA and other statutes refer to url link in the Resources section.

over banks. The result is that your land financing is difficult, if not impossible to obtain, and more costly on every level.

Though you may grit your teeth, don't despair. The wet blanket of regulations and the paralysis of banks has opened other doors—in many cases involving financing methods and paths far more friendly and lucrative then one could ever obtain from a financial institution, even in the good ol' days! See Chapter 13.

When Bad Becomes Terrible

Back to the nitty-gritty. Here's what happens behind the scenes at your local bank if they currently have a land loan of any type on the books, or you've submitted a loan request to acquire land. The land must be self-supporting and you must have the financial wherewithal and credit to carry the property as if there is not a penny of income. The LTV must be 50% or less, in some hard-hit economic locations 40% or less. Exceptional credit purchasers of larger production tracts might be able to raise LTV to 60% or 70%. The appraisal process has become a nightmare. Even the most qualified appraisers are regarded with a jaundiced eye. More often than not, review appraisals[2] will be required, creating additional expense. Appraisals, and the new definitions of "conforming property", as it now applies to the comparable properties and sales that appraisers rely on in putting together their appraisal product, is discussed in later in this chapter. You'll shake your head in wonder.

When a bank is visited by bank examiners, (once again I'm not going to let us get sucked down into the weeds) these examiners are from the state if it is a state bank, and from the Federal Deposit Insurance Corporation (FDIC), and Office of the Comptroller of

[2]The bank hires a second appraiser to "re-appraise" and/or review the initial appraisal.

Currency (OCC) if it is a federally chartered bank. These examiners go through most, if not all, of the loan files. Paperwork must be in perfectly proper order. Many of you have received calls from your banker requesting updated financial statements, tax returns, or "this, that or the other" document. That probably means files are being cleaned up in anticipation of a visit by the examiners. In addition to looking at the propriety of the paperwork, the examiners attempt to interpolate current regulations—ever fluid edicts having been handed down from on high—with their opinions of value, income and borrower credit worthiness and cash flow.

Before 2008, although you needed decent credit (unless you were the recipient of a residential subprime mortgage), banks loaned primarily on the asset. Was the value of the asset relative to the loan amount and under the worst conditions, such that the bank comes out of it with no loss? The cash flow, financial statement and other related paperwork were icing on the cake. Now, in the new climate, the asset is no longer the object and focal point of the loan, and carries far less weight than does the borrower and the borrower's cash flow. In an economy where premium cash flow is hard to come by, it is easy to see why this confluence of the new regulatory environment and land finance has collided in a terrible wreck.

If a loan has not performed perfectly, i.e., there have been any delays in payments, the examiners "think" the market is changing, the bank has other problem loans which make all loans suspect and a host of other reasons, the file is flagged. Discussions take place between the bank and the examiners as to how to handle the files. Some files are simply flagged and left for review at the next examination. Others are "classified." In simplest terms, classification means an asset is not performing, or underperforming. If you had to rearrange a loan structure with a lending institution in which interest rates were lowered, principal payments were deferred, or virtually anything not exactly like the original loan documents was negotiated, this loan is probably now viewed as underperforming. Nonperforming means nothing at all is being paid.

Tightening the Regulatory Noose

There are five levels of classification, "pass, special mention, substandard, doubtful and loss." Level I, which is called a "pass", is the least onerous. Level five, "loss", is most severe. Under current regulations, any classification from pass and downwards, requires the bank to take a certain portion of its capital—in simplest terms its equity in its business—and reserve against it. Since banks can make loans based on a percentage of their capital, this frozen portion of the capital means they can make fewer loans. Less loans means no financing for you, and decreased profitability for the bank. At level five, loss, the reserve is 100% of the loan amount. You can see how a smaller bank, if the examiners have classified a number of loans at levels four or five, can suddenly have less capital than regulations require. That's when a bank "fails" and is taken over.

A Dark History—Now Repeating
How Your Money Funds Guaranteed Profits to Others

When the Savings & Loans (S&L) ran into this problem in the early and mid-1980s the assets of failed thrifts which is virtually everything and includes all loans—were transferred to the "Acquirer". The Acquirer is the bank that stepped into the shoes of the failed S&L. In those days, thirty years ago, the "broker" was the Federal Savings and Loan Insurance Corporation (FSLIC). A shell bank was set up called the "bad" bank. Loans that would not pay off, or were not paying in full in the estimation of the regulators, went to the bad bank. Loans that were performing went to the good bank, i.e., the reconstituted savings and loan which had been acquired by the Acquirer.[3]

Later, the government set up a new layer, the RTC, or Resolution Trust Corporation, which in effect was a shell that cloaked the FDIC, the "real party in interest."

The process is now administered directly by the FDIC. Many of you have likely already experienced the failure of a lender. Many more of you will. I am currently involved in two separate situations involving failed lenders. They are not any fun. Many times, the people of the failed bank with whom you have developed relationships with over the years are gone, replaced by persons you've never seen or heard of, who must get approval for everything from the acquiring bank, which may be one thousand miles distant, not even a real estate bank, has never seen the land and surely knows nothing about your market area. The acquiring bank is driven strictly by an agreement called the Loss Share Agreement between it and the FDIC. It is *guaranteed* a significant profit if it follows the agreement. The Acquirer will make no moves, no matter how sound for the land, collateral, tax payers and others, if such action interferes with the Loss Share Agreement. When I tell you why, you will be less than pleased.

Guaranteed Profit—From *YOUR* Pocket

The sordid truth is that the acquiring bank has purchased the assets of the failing bank at a significant discount. However, the

[3]Additionally, Acquirers were generally paid a management fee for so-called supervision of the assets of the "Bad Bank".

FDIC, through the Loss Share Agreement has guaranteed the acquiring bank face value of the assets.

Additionally, the acquiring bank is insulated completely from all cost and loss. That means the acquiring bank and its legal counsel have carte blanche to spend taxpayer money. So long as they follow the edicts of the Loss Share Agreement—which typically restricts just about any common sense business approach to handling real estate, lending, assets and borrowers—not only are they guaranteed no loss, they are guaranteed a profit. That profit is a difference between what they purchased the assets for and the face amount of the assets.

Let's say you have a $500,000 loan. Your bank fails, and is taken over by an Acquirer via a Loss Share Agreement. The Acquirer purchased your $500,000 loan for somewhere between $250,000 and $400,000. Whatever steps it takes, or does not take, and all the costs and expenses associated with those steps, or lack of steps, will be reimbursed to it by FDIC—which is *you,* the taxpayer. At the end of the day with all costs covered, no risk—and no reward if prudent business practices are followed—the acquiring bank will get $500,000 even though it paid far less for the asset. The difference is paid by you, the taxpayer.

It does not take a Ph.D. in economics to understand that there is no incentive whatsoever for an Acquirer, or the FDIC, to do anything. The same is true for their attorneys. The attorneys basically feed off an annuity, which is the United States Treasury. That the lack of application of common sense in a situation like this will hurt the surrounding market area, thereby further crippling the value of the portfolio of the Acquirer—or other banks—seems to make no difference. That, with time, an asset has plenty of value and could pay off everyone in full including profit, saving the tax payers any cost, means nothing. That the advance of a small amount of money for improvements which would create additional operational cash flow, which would in turn cover the debt service during the holding period, is not relevant. The effect on the rest of the market or the real value of the real estate has absolutely no bearing on the decisions, or lack of decisions made.

Those of you who have experienced this unfortunate situation know that whatever agreements the failed bank had with you, particularly if verbal, mean nothing to the acquiring bank and the FDIC. You've entered a brave new world where business sense has no footing or worth, and—as has been admitted directly to me—the borrower, the taxpayer, the asset, the market, the stability of other banks with loans in the market, all come second to the acquiring bank's adherence to Loss Share Agreement (its ticket to guaranteed fat profits). In summation, the acquiring bank is guaranteed a profit, piggybacked on the borrower's equity in the land or real estate, all paid for by the United States taxpayer.

At least the rape and pillage inherent to the old FSLIC Assistance Agreements is a bit less. Discounts of 10 to 60%, via the Loss Share, though still incredible, are better than some of the deals made "way back when." I am personally familiar with a FSLIC deal in which a $27 billion thrift was acquired by a wealthy family from Texas. There was purportedly $9 billion in nonperforming assets that went to the "bad bank." The other $17 to $18 billion in performing assets went to the acquiring bank. For that $17 billion in assets, this family paid $100 million. They were paid millions per month to manage the bad bank, which was a shell with no—zero—employees. The FSLIC Assistance Agreement in that case even provided forgiveness of up to $50 million in fraudulent management of these assets every three years. I wish I was making this up, but I'm not. More on this amazing story in Volume Two.

What does all this mean to you as a purchaser of land? Do some research on the bank to which you apply for, or have, a loan. If you're caught in the unfortunate quandary as described above, subsequent volumes of *Land for Love and Money* will give you some ideas and cold hard strategies to employ in your attempts to extricate yourself from a morass not of your own doing.

This all brings us to the silver lining in the sorry state of lending affairs. There are bright rays of sunshine in the darkest clouds. As dire as the current conventional finance situation is for land buyers there is a way to turn these financing obstacles to your advantage, whether you are a buyer or seller of land. It doesn't involve the government, the banks, overbearing regulations, and it's as flexible as you and the other guy at the table want to make it.

Chapter Ten
The Brave New World and the Big "Gotcha"
The Appraisal—It Can Blow Your Deal or Cost You Cash

Appraisals have always been important to real estate lending, and valuation but with the avalanche of regulations descending upon property ownership, purchase, sale, realty work, and banking, appraisals have become critical.

There are very few appraisers that do not have distinctive professional designations.[1] There are many levels of appraisal designations, and appraisers wear their badges proudly. Some of the most common are:

- MAI, Member of Appraisal Institute
- SRA, Senior Residential Appraiser
- ARA, Accredited Rural Appraiser

The great majority of appraisers are hard-working, conscientious, conduct intensive research, have an extensive intelligence network, travel incessantly, and put in long hours. As with any industry, there are always a few bad apples. The government, in its zeal to protect us all and expand its swath of control, has instituted regulations via the new financial regulatory laws, which in certain cases can make appraisers liable for "bad" appraisals. Fines start at $10,000.

[1]For detailed information on appraiser designations and changing appraisal requirements, see url links in the Resources section.

Various segments and locations of real estate markets each have their own peculiarities. Any appraiser can do the paper research necessary to do an appraisal. In my opinion, the only real appraisals are by appraisers who specialize in specific types of real estate, have built a network for market intelligence (which becomes part of the appraisal), are conversant in localized market trends (which can affect realistic assessments of value and perceptions of demand) and go out and kick the dirt. Appraising a house is a whole different animal than appraising an acreage, and even further removed from a farm and ranch appraisal. Appraisers consider all aspects of the property: location, type, amenities, income and replacement cost. Appraisals are sometimes predicated on the estimated completed value of a structure from plans (i.e., not yet built) or, a piece of land "as improved" (improvements to be completed in the future tense). These valuations are used to project pricing based on completion of future improvements.

New regulations have greatly tightened what appraisers can use for "comparables". Comparables, also referred to as "comps", are properties similar to the property being appraised, located in the immediate or "like market" areas. The new regulations that govern appraisals due to so-called financial regulatory reforms include both tweaks and substantial changes to methodology that an appraiser may employ. As a few examples:

- comparable property sales must be closed within last 12 months
- appraiser must note any nonconforming aspects of the property
- appraiser must, where possible, discard the highest and lowest of their comparables

IMPORTANT! Listings (unsold properties) *don't* count. *Only* properties sold and closed may be used as a comparable.

Currently, a combination of regulations and lender policies dictate that there must be a minimum number of comparables. Under the new guidelines, log and certain other homes are "nonconforming." More on this later in the chapter. Guidelines and regulations are definitely geared to the typical exurban, suburban and in-city real estate. Finally, comparables of rural property are subject to distance restrictions (often a "comp" must be within a mile, five miles or seven miles of the appraisal property). This can be problematic when your nearest neighbor is more than seven miles away.

Understand that your final loan approval, no matter what type of commitment letter you think you have, is always subject to the appraisal. And the bank will loan only a certain percentage, the LTV, of the final appraisal value. A low appraisal can blow your budgeting, or the deal, to the four winds.

Let's assume you are buying a piece of land, with a home, for a purchase price of $300,000. The buyer has, of course, told you what a terrific deal you're getting and how they can barely let it go for that price. Your realtor has enthusiastically assured you—and believes—that this is a great value for the market. You budget a 20% down payment, ($60,000) and plan to borrow 80% ($240,000) of the purchase price. Everyone assumes that there will be no problem with the appraisal, which will come in at least at $300,000 or more.

The appraisal does come back at $300,000 but the review appraiser, who typically never sees the property and just works off paper, determines the proper valuation is $280,000. Or, perhaps the initial appraisal comes in below the purchase price. The buyers and sellers now have a quandary. If the contract is written properly, either can walk, and the earnest money will be refunded to the buyer. The contract should also provide for the parties to get together when a problem like this arises to see if they can work it out prior to either party electing to terminate.

Let's assume, in our example that the sellers are unwilling to lower the price to conform to the appraisal. A lesser price would obviously take care of the buyer's problem, but could adversely affect the seller's budget, or, as is often the case in the current economy, might not generate enough cash for the seller to pay off the debt on the property because values have fallen. In this case, you, the buyer, have a decision to make. If you really love the property, it speaks to you, and it works on many different levels for all aspects of your life, you might proceed with the purchase. However, your loan amount can now not exceed the approved LTV, let's use 80% of $280,000. If the buyer sticks to their $300,000 sale price you will be taking $16,000 more out of your pocket to complete the closing.[2] Over the past several years, these types of situations have become more prevalent, so this possibility needs to be kept in mind.

The appraisal "gotcha" also affects sellers. You can price a property at whatever you wish, but it's unlikely to appraise at that higher value if the property miraculously does sell. So, any contract that does come in will probably not close. A buyer, after investing the time and emotional energy to decide to purchase, to write a contract, negotiate that document, and begin to jump through the hoops of obtaining financing, will not be pleased. You, as the seller, will have lost valuable marketing time, particularly critical to rural properties that show far better in the spring, summer and early fall months, than in late fall and winter.

[2]You might possibly raise the LTV, but your interest rate will increase, and you may be saddled with additional monthly mortgage insurance premiums charged for higher LTV rations.

I have a colloquialism I like to invoke, which unfortunately I have not always followed. There will be several stories of the resulting disasters further in this, and future volumes. *Pigs are fat and happy, and hogs get slaughtered.* In other words, it's okay to negotiate hard and smart for the best possible price, but if you get greedy, bad things will happen, the least of which is losing the sale.

Don't Be a Non-Conformist

There are other interesting and frustrating wrinkles in the new appraisal guidelines. One of the most onerous is the evolving definition for "conforming property." The list of properties that "conform" in the minds of whoever dreams up this stuff is shrinking. Certain types of foundations no longer qualify for mortgage financing, cinderblock in many locations being one example. Log homes, though always in a special class, are no longer considered conforming. That should prove rather distressing to the million or so people who own log homes. Certain types of water supply systems, septic treatment systems, access roads, distances from fire departments, even rural fire departments, can throw a loan (on land that contains structures or a residence) into the "nonconforming" class. The result is an immediate decrease in the value of these properties, and huge, sometimes insurmountable hurdles for sellers who suddenly own nonconforming real estate. A nightmare of financing complexities arise for the buyer. Appraisers are being told to discount the value of such properties. The fact is most lenders won't touch them, unless perhaps via a short-term commercial loan, and even then reluctantly.

* * * * *

This true story will drive home the point. Just in the past several years I took on a client as a buyer's agent. She was looking for rural property twenty to thirty miles from a university town in the Rockies. The purchaser was eminently qualified—perhaps golden in this day and age—virtually no debt, excellent credit, enough money for the down payment and a secure, high-paying job. She had no real estate to sell so she was not tethered to the past. We found a beautiful, twenty-four-hundred square foot cabin needing completion on forty acres, with a creek, privacy, surrounded by large ranches, within the commuting distance she wished, and all at the right price. She was prequalified for her mortgage.

She cut a good deal with a pleased seller who had been trying to sell his property for a year. Then came the process of attempting to convert her prequalified mortgage into a loan for closing. The first obstacle was a limitation on acreage. No mortgage lender would touch the deal if it was over eight acres. I was familiar with this "gotcha" and a surveyor quickly surveyed a mortgage exemption parcel[3] of eight acres. Ah! Problem solved! Not so much.

Shortly before her contract, log homes had been relegated from their specific class to "non-conforming." I was not aware of this "down grade". Because the home was log, several mortgage companies turned it down flat. One other company said they would consider it at a greater cost and higher interest rate, but they had to have three comparables within seven miles—an obvious impossibility in a rural area having few homes, fewer still log structures, and very few sales, in fact, virtually no properties on the market. Finally, at my

[3]A survey that is for mortgage purposes only, may not be sold separately, and under the laws of most states is not a subdivision.

suggestion, she approached a commercial bank. The best the bank could do was a five-year, short-term loan at an onerous interest-rate for this day and age, and only if they slapped a hefty 30 to 40% down payment on the table. The bank never really clarified how much. They were less than enthusiastic about tackling the deal.

Everything else about this property was sterling—access, location, the home itself (despite needing mostly interior completion) and the land was a gem. The hoops she had to jump through, to no avail, and the approximate $4,000 she spent on due diligence on the property—checking the well, septic, having it surveyed, were all for naught. She even went to the expense of having an architect draw up plans for finishing the interior of the residence because the commercial bank said it couldn't consider the financing without drawings. That was more than a year ago. The poor seller, a terrific older gentleman, still owns the property and has taken it off the market. He didn't want to seller finance. It will be impossible to sell except to a cash buyer.

My client subsequently found a different acreage property, which she also fell in love with and purchased, and with a brick home. The same mortgage lenders that refused to loan on the log home, tripped over themselves competing for my client's business on their second choice.

If you are a seller, investigate any aspects of your property that might be nonconforming. Talk to an appraiser and a realtor in your local area. Fix these non-conforming aspects if you can, or plan to hold the property for quite some time. Alternatively, put together a plan with your realtor and advisors to offer seller financing.

If you are a buyer, query your realtor thoroughly on conforming and nonconforming properties, which like just about everything else in this environment of increasing regulations, continues to mutate to the disadvantage of buyers, sellers and real estate markets. Understand that rural property is far more likely to have some nonconforming aspect than a typical urban or suburban residence. Whether or not these expanding definitions of nonconforming tie into the stated objectives of Agenda 21 (discussed in Chapter 12), or are just a coincidence, remains to be seen.

Just as buyers "forget the shovel" or fail to plan prior to purchase for value enhancements to their land and property, so to do sellers often fall short on thinking about the big picture and forecasting ahead.

"A Little Dab Will Do Ya" Goes a Long Way

Sellers need to clean up their property and land prior to the appraisers making their visit. This is just common sense, but it's amazing how many sellers simply don't get this basic principle. Everyone knows what needs be done to make a house look presentable. When you're selling a piece of land, or acreage that includes a residential structure, at least fix the fences so that they are not falling down. Be sure the entry is clean and trimmed. Pick up trash, haul off, or at least arrange, older vehicles. Get equipment inside or lined up so that it appears you are organized. A fresh coat of paint, or oil, fixing the hole in the barn roof, spraying, or at least cutting, wild jungles of weed patches readily visible from the roads or structures, cleaning out barns and stalls, and painting that weathered sign at the entry, all add up to a significant visual and subliminal affect, not only in the minds of the appraiser, but in the eyes of potential buyers and their realtors. The nice thing about getting a property presentable for an appraisal is that the tasks are exactly the same as preparing a property for a tour by a buyer and their agent, or your realtor and potential co-brokers (who, if impressed, will greatly expand your network of potential purchasers). If you are selling a vehicle, you certainly would not leave it covered in mud and un-vacuumed before a potential buyer came to inspect, would you?

Because the appraisal will be such a key element to your buyer's financing and therefore actually closing a purchase and sale contract, time and attention is required if you're going to sell your property. This bit of work will contribute to both a higher price and, even if incremental, to a higher appraised value.

Land Appraisals—Certain Advantages

There are some legitimate, real-life value increase mechanisms available to you as the buyer or financer of land that a strictly residential property does not enjoy. An appraisal can be based on many things. If your land is production ground, on which there is or can be very quantifiable and specific improvements that will create a solid stream of revenue, your loan request should be heavily weighted toward valuing the property based on its income. Sometimes the income from land, when interpolated for valuation as a ratio called the capitalization rate (CAP Rate), can create a higher value than could be justified by the acreage alone.

Most appraisals of land are completed based on the "highest and best use" approach to market valuation. The smaller the acreage, the higher the per-acre price or value will be. An appraisal of a thousand-acre ranch could quite legitimately be boosted if the evaluation was made of portions of the ranch and then aggregated for final value on the whole property. Though most don't realize it, many large tracts have what I term, "old deeds." These are prior subdivisions, or parcels that may have been created or purchased long ago, remainders from sections, and a host of other existing tracts. Each state has different laws, but the upfront research of the title to the property going back to the very beginning, might be well worth the effort and expense. This can usually be accomplished by ordering an "abstract", which unlike a title commitment (summary of current title condition of the property), is a compendium of the entire history of the property title. More times than not, a review of the abstract by a competent attorney and surveyor will unearth nuggets that will prove valuable to you on many levels during your course of ownership. It may likely reveal old deeds, i.e., tracts existing as of the date of your purchase that could be severed without any governmental review and sold separately from the whole. If you plan the grant of conservation easements, these pre-existing severable parcels can increase donative value considerably.

If you can prove the existence of the old deeds via the abstract examination, then it may well be that the value of the property in parts may be greater than the value of the property as a whole. So long as the backup is concrete, references made to that approach in the loan request package you furnish the lender, will then be conveyed to the appraiser, and the appraisal value may rise.

Different portions of your land may have quite dissimilar characteristics. Parts may be flat, treeless and dry. Other areas may have a creek or pond. There may be areas with another spectacular feature or view. Portions may be irrigated.

In these cases, the appraisal can be based on the various types of land. The land is separated into zones, then the values of the zones are aggregated into one overall appraisal. I have seen lands in different zones on the same ranch very properly differ in value by as much as

$5,000 per acre using this methodology which generally results in a higher valuation than for a single value derived from a blanket appraisal.

*****

Back in 1999–2000, I got together with a number of folks and formed an LLC. We purchased a two-thousand-acre ranch. Extensive agricultural and resource improvements were planned for the ranch, and the group wished to preserve critical portions of it in perpetuity through the grants of conservation easements. Extensive research was done, including an abstract examination that was reviewed by both legal counsel and a qualified local surveyor. We found, much to our surprise, that there existed more than thirty "old deeds" on this two-thousand-acre ranch, ranging from five to sixty acres. To make doubly sure these existing tracts, which existed from long before, could be sold by us or anyone else owning the ranch to individual purchasers, (and therefore had value) we requested and received an opinion from the state Attorney General, that stated in synopsis: "Yes, indeed these old tracts exist, they were pre-existing, and they are salable." With that blessing in hand, the donative value of the conservation easements, and overall real value of the ranch increased significantly.

There are exceptions to every rule but it is unusual to find a piece of land larger than twenty to forty acres that does not have some type of similar "value realization opportunity" hidden either somewhere in the fascinating story of title since its first ownership, or in its varying physical features.

*****

Under the new regulations you don't get to choose the appraiser for your property. That selection is made by the bank. The bank must submit a written request for appraisal to the appraiser of their choice. In rural areas, you may be dealing with a small or midsize bank hundreds of miles away. They may ask for suggestions, generally requesting two, three or four names who they will then investigate before deciding who to hire. With the recent rules, I've personally seen deals where the more local bank is mandated to use certain appraisers by a far removed regional or national office. Their appraisers may live and perform most of their work hundreds of miles from your land. They know very little about the local market in which your parcel is located, and they don't have the network of realtors, buyers and sellers. These can be difficult situations. On the other hand, with the current surreal extreme limitations on land-related finance, "He who has the gold, writes the rules."

The screws began to tighten on the appraisal industry with sweeping financial regulation known as FIRREA.[4] The guidelines, edicts and constraints have multiplied exponentially in the last three years, and will most likely continue to mutate. You can rest assured appraisals will become more important and more difficult in the future.

The moral of this chapter? If you are a buyer, don't purchase machinery to do all those value adding improvements you have planned for your land, or schedule a moving van, prior to the appraisal being completed. If you are a seller, it is recommended you not sell your furniture, or rent or purchase the place where you plan to move—unless you are able to extricate yourself from the deal—until the appraisal on the property you are selling is complete.

[4]See Resources section for url link to further information.

Chapter Eleven
Pigs Are Fat and Happy—Hogs Get Slaughtered

Now let's discuss the reality of being a seller in today's environment. By this point in *Land for Love and Money,* we have reached four conclusions together:

1) There are macro forces beyond our control—economic, market, and regulatory;
2) Land and real estate are affairs of both the heart and the wallet;
3) The math is the math; and
4) Land is a long term asset—planning should occur before the closing.

As a seller, you must consider what the cost of carrying your land asset is. *All the costs.* There are administrative and maintenance expenses related to your land. There may be other operating costs. There are taxes and insurance. If you have debt, you're paying interest. These costs and cash outflows add up quickly. I have been told many times by realtors that the best offer you'll ever receive on your property is the very first one. I'm not sure I subscribe to that theory, but I'm a big believer in unemotional cost-benefit analysis when you do get an offer on a property that you wish to, need to or must sell.

Let's say you have had a property listed for one or two years—not all that uncommon in the current economic climate. You, or you and your realtor, have tried different marketing ploys. Perhaps you have reduced the price once, or more.

Finally, a buyer tours the property, and instead of the objections and excuses that you've heard from all the other folks who've been on the land and kicked the tires, you are delighted to hear the words, "I like it. I'm going to make an offer." Let's assume you're not locked into a sales price because anything less means an underwater closing, i.e., having to bring money to the table to divest yourself of the asset. The eagerly anticipated offer comes in lower than you contemplated and certainly lower than you wished—another common occurrence in today's economy. As you ponder and think about the offer within the timeframe permitted by the contract, you begin to convince yourself you can get more, the property is worth more, the market is turning, neighbor Joe got "XYZ" for his property, and yours is better and so on. Sound familiar?

There's almost always some wiggle room in offers, both ways. In today's climate, there are other properties this buyer can purchase, though in your egocentric view these properties are not as nice, nothing quite like yours. In some cases, that's true. In most cases, it is not.

You wrestle with reality and then tell your realtor, "The offer pisses me off. It's insulting. Tell them it's rejected. I'm not going to counter." Take a deep breath. Again there's always exceptions, but I will tell you that only in the rarest of occasions in my forty year career, have I ever further pursued a deal where an offer was rejected, rather than countered. It tells me something about the seller, and it's annoying when I took my time, and invested energy and effort to investigate the property, construct the offer in good faith, and submit it. Many people think like I do.

A very wise, eighty-eight-year old superstar realtor told me about another broker to whom she had presented an offer. The listing agent glanced quickly at the price, looked up and snapped, "This is a very disappointing offer."

My friend replied, "Think about how disappointing no offer would have been."

It's *always* better to counter. When you counter, take a deep breath and think. Sure the offer may make you clench your jaw, but you can probably sneak out a few more bucks per acre. It is rare—though not unheard of—that the first offer from a sincere buyer does not have some upside wiggle room, albeit perhaps small.

Get out your pen and paper. What is the absolute bottom dollar you'll take for this piece of real estate? Does accepting the offer adversely affect any land you are retaining? What about appraisals on the rest of your land? This sale could become a comp. If you accept the offer, what is the cost of moving? Are there any other costs associated with selling the property that will not be on the closing settlement statement?

Now perform the exercise in reverse. If you don't take the offer, or make a greedy counteroffer and the buyer walks, what if the next buyer doesn't walk in the door for another year or two? (You may think this unlikely, but it is always a possibility.) What will it cost you to hold the property if the market doesn't move much over that time period and the property rises only minimally in value? How much will you leave on the table by not getting a deal done now? There's a time value to money. There is greater value to your time. If you have greener pastures to move to, financial, spiritual, or personal, what's the price your heart will pay if you are delayed?

If the deal is strictly financial or mostly financial, then it's simple. Let's do an example with easy numbers. You have a property you want to sell for $100,000. There is a $50,000 loan on the property. You are paying 6% interest. Taxes, insurance, and other annual property costs are $5,000. You get an offer for $80,000—the best the buyer will do. If you don't take the offer and the property sells two years from now at your asking price ($20,000 more than the current offer), you will have spent $16,000 (2 x $3,000 + 2 x $5,000) to get to that final sale—"netting" only $4,000 more. If inflation is 2.5% a year the $80,000 is decreasing in real money terms by $2,000 each annum. Two years out that $80,000 now will purchase only $76,000 of today's goods and services. If you take the current $80,000 offer, you move on toward the life direction you have chosen for yourself, and you pick up two years on your plans, for a cost of $4,000 *before* inflation. If the inflation rate was zero, (it's not) is a year of your life worth $2,000?

* * * * *

Here's a real life example. One of the rare clients for whom I act as buyer's agent is a wealthy, high income individual. He's been looking at ranch properties for several years. More than two years ago, we looked at a terrific ranch in excess of ten thousand unimproved acres in a western state. We will refer to the property as Ranch "A." We spent a full day on the property, got a preliminary handle on what types of improvements could be done and where, put together a rough game plan on partial conservation easement grants that he needs to shelter his income, and which he believes in his heart is the right thing to do. We met with the seller, got along well, and several days later I submitted an offer on the buyer's behalf. At that time, the seller wanted about $14 million for the property. He had turned down a $12 million offer several months prior. The proverbial *caca* was beginning to hit the economic fan, and the Great Recession was gathering a full head of steam.

After some back and forth, my client offered $10.5 million. The seller countered at slightly under $14 million. My client had decided he would not pay more than $11 million based on comparable sales, the amount he would have to expend to create the types of resource improvements that he wanted for recreation purposes, and other factors. The two minds never met and the deal never got done.

Flash forward to 2012. After several years of looking at more places, my client decided he wanted to take another run at the place that had always intrigued him the most, Ranch "A." I had several discussions with the listing broker. There were other terms and conditions—some of them critical to my client—that the seller refused to budge on. Mostly stubborn I presumed, because as a seller I would have not had a problem with them at all, although perhaps I might have massaged the details just a bit. My client offered some clever terms, which in essence was a $7 million base price but $8.5 million give or take in the end to the seller. The seller countered at $10.2 million, ironically about the amount my client had offered three years prior.

In the end it was a repeat of the prior experience. The seller wouldn't budge or give. I had done the research for my client as to value, and comparable sales. He felt his offer was fair and was not pleased that the seller continued to refuse a few of the nonfinancial aspects of the deal. The seller still owns that ranch.

Had he sold for $10.5 million three years ago, and assuming

that he invested the funds, let's say in tax free municipal bonds at a 7+/-% return, his income on the money received would have totaled $2.1+/- million. The cost of keeping a property of this size in that particular location is not less than $50,000 a year. Other than leasing pasture, the property has no income. Another $150,000 in costs. Tax rates may be changing on capital gains. If the capital gains rate increases even 10%, it's an additional approximate $1 million cost to the seller. If inflation is 2.5% (many feel it is currently over 10%), the purchasing power of his dollars decreased about $250,000 a year. That's another $750,000. There is a $240,000 decrease in commission to the Realtors at a 6% commission rate on the lower price, *and* a decrease in capital gains tax at 15% on the approximate $4 million *face* amount of price decrease—a savings of yet another $600,000!

Basically, had the seller done the deal three years ago he would have been free to move on—energized by the sale and his future dreams, and removing uncertainty from his life equation. His total financial benefit, including the risk of increased capital gain tax, the opportunity cost of money even if invested at a paltry 7%, plus the savings in operating costs and considering inflation, would have been the equivalent of a current $14 million sales price.

Perhaps the seller will now get $10.2 million at some point from someone. I wish him well. The fact of the matter is, he's lost three years and left a minimum of $3.7 million or more on the table due to the delay.

Pigs are fat and happy. Hogs get slaughtered.

Chapter Twelve
We Are from the Government, and We Are Here to Help You. *NOT!*

Whichever side of the political spectrum you're on, there's widespread agreement that there is more government, and more regulation. These rules from on high, and to a lesser but noticeable extent, flowing from state and local governments, affect land, real estate in general, and your purchase, sale, ownership and improvement of these assets in direct and indirect ways. We've discussed some thus far, but it's impossible to review all in a few chapters or one book. Some regulations, like Dodd-Frank, could justify a volume all by themselves. This chapter is intended to give you a feel for trends, what's "big" in this ever connecting, ever thickening ganglion of rules which affect, or could affect your land.

The Folks Outside of America—How They Feel About Your Land

From Agenda 21: "*Private Property Ownership is the primary cause of Social Injustice*"—United Nations—UN.org[1]

The United Nations Conference on Environment and Development (UNCED) held in Rio de Janeiro, Brazil, in 1992 was the start of "Agenda 21." This forty-chapter, ever-evolving bible

[1]For official United Nations and other links to all forty chapters (four sections) please see Resources section in the back of this volume.

of globalism is divided into four sections: (I) Social and Economic Dimensions, (II) Conservation and Management of Resources for Development, (III) Strengthening the Role of Major Groups, (IV) Means of Implementation.

Warm, fuzzy language, ambiguous or general in meaning was, and is cleverly used, first to get one hundred and seventy plus sovereign nations to sign on in 1992—including the United States[2]—and over the last decade of "implementation" to sift into and permeate governments and government policies at Federal, regional and local levels worldwide, the United States included. There are those who get lost in the feel good "sustainability, poverty, education" language and are inclined to dismiss any thought of a more sinister intent directed at the sovereignty of nation states, or individual freedoms around the globe. Are we are misreading the words or intent? Here is a summary—again from the Agenda 21 Treatise itself:

> *Effective execution of Agenda 21 will require a profound reorientation of all human society, unlike anything the world has ever experienced a major shift in the priorities of both governments and individuals and an unprecedented redeployment of human and financial resources. This shift will demand that a concern for the environmental consequences of every human action be integrated into individual and collective decision-making at every level.*

I believe that—putting aside the fuzzy mask of feel good words that few could argue with if used in the normal context—a careful reading of Agenda 21, and all other documents ancillary to Agenda 21, all prepared by or under the auspices of the UN, are revealing

[2]This matter transcends presidents and parties, though implementation at various levels of American government has accelerated over the past four years.

and support the excerpts above. The essence of Agenda 21 is indeed that the root of social injustice is the ownership of land.[3]

The problem is not at the local level. The problem lies in the smoke-filled chambers where politicians huddle to cut deals and create ridiculous laws intended to woo this constituency or that, and promote their ideology, and from the stark offices at the highest level of government where regulations enforcing these laws are written by clever, shadowy bureaucrats who sincerely believe bigger government, more regulations and less private is good. It is from these higher levels that the culture trickles down to agencies that then trample the property rights of specific people, classes of people, and landowners. The poor folks at the local Fed level have to operate within this framework. I can tell in my discussions with them that most of them are not pleased with their predicament.

The danger of ambiguous diversionary language is that it is used to power agendas that were not part of the original intention of those who ratified the agreement, and that ambiguous language covers all the bases. In other words, even if you assume this all began with honorable intentions, Agenda 21 has morphed into an international attack on personal property rights everywhere. Here is more from Agenda 21—Core Document. These sections should be read with the bigger picture disclosures revealed above in mind. Those are the core beliefs that drive the rest of the Agenda 21 document.

> "Humanity stands at a defining moment in history. We are confronted with a perpetuation of disparities between and within nations, a worsening of poverty, hunger, ill health

[3]The full text of Agenda 21 can be found on the website of the United Nations itself, UN.org. Links are provided in the Resources section in the back of this volume.

> and illiteracy, and the continuing deterioration of the ecosystems on which we depend for our well-being. However, integration of environment and development concerns and greater attention to them will lead to the fulfillment of basic needs, improved living standards for all, better protected and managed ecosystems and a safer, more prosperous future. No nation can achieve this on its own; but together we can—in a global partnership for sustainable development."
>
> "Agenda 21 is a comprehensive plan of action to be taken globally, nationally and locally by organizations of the United Nations System, Governments, and Major Groups in every area in which human impacts on the environment."

Note: *Every area in which human impacts on the environment.* Wouldn't that be everywhere on the planet?

> "7.27. Access to land resources is an essential component of sustainable low-impact lifestyles. Land resources are the basis for (human) living systems and provide soil, energy, water and the opportunity for all human activity. In rapidly growing urban areas, access to land is rendered increasingly difficult by the conflicting demands of industry, housing, commerce, agriculture, land tenure structures and the need for open spaces. Furthermore, the rising costs of urban land prevent the poor from gaining access to suitable land. In rural areas, unsustainable practices, such as the exploitation of marginal lands and the encroachment on forests and ecologically fragile areas by commercial interests and landless rural populations, result in environmental degradation, as well as

in diminishing returns for impoverished rural settlers."

"The objective is to provide for the land requirements of human settlement development through environmentally sound physical planning and land use so as to ensure access to land to all households and, where appropriate, the encouragement of communally and collectively owned and managed land. Particular attention should be paid to the needs of women and indigenous people for economic and cultural reasons."

"(g) Accelerate efforts to promote access to land by the urban and rural poor, including credit schemes for the purchase of land and for building/acquiring or improving safe and healthy shelter and infrastructure services;"

"(h) Develop and support the implementation of improved land-management practices that deal comprehensively with potentially competing land requirements for agriculture, industry, transport, urban development, green spaces, preserves and other vital needs;"

"(i) Promote understanding among policy makers of the adverse consequences of unplanned settlements in environmentally vulnerable areas and of the appropriate national and local land-use and settlements policies required for this purpose."

Note: Above, they discuss *all* land on the planet. These subsections (g), (h) and (i), seem to reference *every* possible human economic and personal use of land imaginable. Let's peruse a bit more!

> "7.29. All countries should consider, as appropriate, undertaking a comprehensive national inventory of their land resources in order to establish a land information system in which land resources will be classified according to their most appropriate uses and environmentally fragile or disaster-prone areas will be identified for special protection measures."

> "The sustainability of urban development is defined by many parameters relating to the availability of water supplies, air quality and the provision of environmental infrastructure for sanitation and waste management. As a result of the density of users, urbanization, if properly managed, offers unique opportunities for the supply of sustainable environmental infrastructure through adequate pricing policies, educational programs and equitable access mechanisms that are economically and environmentally sound."

Note: Read carefully, given the overall intent of Agenda 21 in its own words on page one and two of this chapter, this appears to assert that on a country by country basis, population should be moved, or forced to move into compact urban areas ("human settlement") from rural areas, especially away from "fragile or disaster prone areas." Who determines that? See Reference page for the link to the UN map of "World Heritage" and "Critical Biosphere" areas in the United States. How could such a stance ever be enforced? They have thought of that, too:

> "Laws and regulations suited to country-specific conditions are among the most important instruments for transforming

environment and development policies into action, not only through 'command and control' methods, but also as a normative framework for economic planning and market instruments. Yet, although the volume of legal texts in this field is steadily increasing, much of the law-making in many countries seems to be ad hoc and piecemeal, or has not been endowed with the necessary institutional machinery and authority for enforcement and timely adjustment."

"8.14. While there is continuous need for law improvement in all countries, many developing countries have been affected by shortcomings of laws and regulations. To effectively integrate environment and development in the policies and practices of each country, it is essential to develop and implement integrated, enforceable and effective laws and regulations that are based upon sound social, ecological, economic and scientific principles. It is equally critical to develop workable programs to review and enforce compliance with the laws, regulations and standards that are adopted. Technical cooperation requirements in this field include legal information, advisory services and specialized training and institutional capacity-building."

"8.15. The enactment and enforcement of laws and regulations (at the regional, national, state/provincial or local/municipal level) are also essential for the implementation of most international agreements in the field of environment and development... The survey of existing agreements... has

[4]The full text of Agenda 21 can be found on the website of the United Nations itself, UN.org. Links are provided in the Resources section in the back of this volume.

> indicated problems of compliance in this respect, and the need for improved national implementation... In developing their national priorities, countries should take account of their international obligations."
>
> "8.16. The overall objective is to promote, in the light of country-specific conditions, the integration of environment and development policies through appropriate legal and regulatory policies, instruments and enforcement mechanisms at the national, state, provincial and local level."

These are rather chilling statements from an organization, the United Nations, to whom the United States gives approximately \$6–\$16 billion in annual support, far more than any other country.[4] International obligations? "Programmes?" "Enforce compliance?" "...local/municipal level?" That seems a bit invasive coming from a global institution. I—and virtually everyone I know involved in land—and many others are all supporters of "sustainable" resources, good "land use", a sparkling "environment" and helping less fortunate folks help themselves. I am a rancher. My life, income, passions and energy flow from the land. But, I have this nagging feeling that our concept of the end game of these objectives, and implementation by free individuals incentivized not only by conviction but because they are owners of and vested in land is wholly different than the grand plan of global authority, control, regulation and implementation envisioned by Agenda 21 and its supporters.

If ownership of property is a foundational cornerstone of liberty and self-reliance here in America, and the price of freedom is vigilance, than we all know what we have to do. Be informed, be aware, and stand shoulder to shoulder with our fellow landowners.

Be particularly observant of any clues that some of these big picture notions are creeping into your state and local government's policies, such as the use of the Agenda 21 buzz words "sustainable", "vision", and "consensus". Whether you are a buyer, seller, owner or manager of land and real estate, the trends in today's world mandate keeping yourself abreast of the actions and thoughts of other folks, within and outside of the United States, who may not share your convictions about the sanctity of private ownership of land and property.

The Feds—Hungry for Your Land and Thirsty for Your Water

We have discussed financial regulations. Perhaps the arc of objectives in Agenda 21, and the federal government's attempts to exercise increasing control over state and local lands, waters, and your private property, is coincidence. However, the undeniable facts are that when bills get blocked in Congress, the result is end-run enforcement actions by the Environmental Protection Agency, (EPA), the United States Department of the Interior (Interior) and the USDA. Let me emphasize that most of the people who work in these bureaucracies at the local level are good, hard-working souls. They care. Many of them strive to make a difference. I have worked with folks on conservation boards, local Farm Service Agency (FSA) and field people from the USDA in countless locations. Only in one case, over decades, did I feel a local conservation board and FSA field office had an ulterior motive.

I'm the EPA—I Must Destroy You to Protect You

The callous rules and regulations of the EPA fill tens of thousands of pages. It is impossible to discuss it all in this book. Here are just some of the highlights, regulations and potential enforcement actions which could affect each and every landowner at some point in time, if they don't already.

Of Critters, Winged Things, Flowers and Fish

The Endangered Species Act (which also includes threatened species, candidate species and critical habitat) is among the most insidious. Which animals, fish or fowl or flora and fauna, are endangered or "threatened" is far less driven by science than by other, far-reaching ulterior motives of environmental groups using the EPA and other federal agencies as their foil to achieve objectives having nothing, or little, to do with the smokescreen of warm, fuzzy critters in danger.

It is no coincidence that many of the "concerns" that arise under the auspices of the Endangered Species Act regarding plants, animals and habitats seem to coincide, when mapped, with some type of actual or planned resource development—the northern spotted owl in the heart of prime Northwest timberlands, the greater sage-grouse throughout the oil and gas discovery zones of western states, the delta smelt, a three inch fish that ventured from the Pacific into irrigation systems in the San Joaquin Valley shutting down almost one hundred thousand acres of one of America's most fertile and productive agricultural regions, to name just a few.

The result is not only restrictive policies that affect private parties, but a general cessation of resource utilization on federal lands that are owned by all of us. While some protections are good, virtually all have been carried far forward of reasonable, affecting value, use, and infringing on private property rights. The administration of these regulations is cumbersome, snail-like, and sometimes politically motivated. And, unfortunately, Section 10 of the Endangered Species

Act, which provides for proactive cooperative Habitat Conservation Plans—similar to conservation easements but without the perpetual commitment of property, is largely ignored.

* * * * *

Several years ago, we designed a pond on one of our Wyoming Ranches as part of our overall, multifaceted resource and agricultural improvements plan. The location was perfect, the water source excellent, and the water rights completely owned by the ranch. As I have recommended in this book, the pond was esthetic, created a fishery, allowed for upland grass utilization by livestock, provided water to several previously dry pastures, was used to augment irrigation, and contributed to wildlife values. It was properly designed and fully permitted by the necessary Wyoming agencies. In the review process, the U.S. Fish and Wildlife Service (USFWS) determined that this area could be prime habitat for the Preble's meadow jumping mouse. Putting aside that there's only been four specimens in the history of mankind of what might be that species, and half the biologists involved believed they were simply four mice with extraordinarily large heads, potential Preble's meadow jumping mouse habitat, combined with greater sage-grouse habitat, is now interfering with improvements, oil, gas and other resource extraction, and other plans in many of the Rocky Mountains states.

USFWS was supposed to do a review and field visit. A month stretched into two, then four, then six. The contractors that had been scheduled to work on the pond got busy with other projects. Cost of the construction was increasing. The benefits to the ranch described above were delayed, in the case of agriculture resulting in a reduced crop yield. I finally called the USFWS administrator in charge of

Preble's meadow jumping mouse habitat. The conversation went something like this:

"I called to inquire as to the status of a release on the permit for a pond on the Laprele Creek Ranch, which the Agency has said might be Preble's meadow jumping mouse habitat."

Her voice was icy. "We have a number of pending applications for those types of projects in potential Preble's meadow jumping mouse habitat areas. They are being processed in order."

I was annoyed. "What exactly do we need to do to get this done? We have been waiting seven months."

"We need to come up and inspect the pond location to see if there are any Preble's meadow jumping mice."

"When might that be?" I snapped.

"Sometime this year," she answered, her tone smug and matter of fact.

Now I was exasperated, "This application has been pending for months, it's now June. Sometime this year could be another six or seven months. Are there any indications that there's ever been a Preble's meadow jumping mouse found in this location or anywhere near this location?"

"No, but it's possible," she said stubbornly.

"So is the sky falling?" (She didn't appreciate that comment much.) "Out of curiosity, if you find a Preble's meadow jumping mouse, what do you do then?"

"We would have to do a necropsy to make sure that it is a Preble's meadow jumping mouse, of course." Her tone was condescending. *These ranchers—I have to explain everything to them.*

I paused as her words sank in and then asked incredulously, "You mean to tell me that you're delaying the work of hundreds if not thousands of people, on hundreds of properties, on tens of thousands of acres, because the area might 'potentially' be habitat for a species that may not exist, and if you find one, you're going to kill it to do a necropsy?"

"Yes."

Fueled by that absurd conversation, I climbed the chain of command and we managed to jolt loose the permit for the pond about thirty days later. USFWS never did inspect.

A friend of mine who has a farm in Idaho was slapped and shut down by the EPA because his dry land farming operation of several generations now, suddenly, "raised too much dust." Based on my experience, running a tractor over dirt with a plow raises dust. He got the situation resolved but not until after he had lost a full planting season.

A More Down to Earth Agency

The U.S. Army Corps of Engineers exercises jurisdiction over certain resource matters too, particularly perennial—year-round—streams and rivers. The Army Corps has many great accomplishments, but they began to overreach in the 2000s. In 2009, a major federal lawsuit determined that they did not have the jurisdiction they claimed to have over spring sources, and non-perennial—intermittent or seasonal—streams. In the Army Corps' defense I have worked with them on several occasions. They have employed common sense, and permits were processed very quickly in emergency situations, including one on the Big Hole River back in 1997, a historic flood year. The river threatened improvements and a cabin owned by one of our clients. The Army Corps, much to its credit, processed the permit in forty-eight hours, allowing work to begin which in the end actually benefited stream habitat, and saved the structures.

There Are Some Rules That Work Too

Some regulations, if properly written, and employed with common sense by knowledgeable local people, have benefit. A state-level statute known as the 310 Law, existing in many states and with several different variations and nomenclatures, prohibits landowners from disturbing or altering the stream bank or streambed without the proper plans, study, permitting and inspection by local agencies. Given the dire downstream effects to the entire basin if somebody is mucking around in a river or creek, this is a regulation that makes sense. It's generally applied with common sense, though there are exceptions.

Ever Spreading Federal Tentacles

But the cascade of regulations coming out of Washington D.C. usurp local control, delay, shut down, and scuttle good projects, and in extreme cases can result in litigation, fines, and penalties. The federal government, especially over the last three or four years, has attempted to greatly broaden its reach in a number of areas. Here are some concerns:

Thirsty? Too Bad

Just before this book went to print, the Department of Interior wrote a letter to Tombstone, Arizona forbidding them from reconstructing their damaged water systems except with a pick and shovel. Julie Decker of the Interior Department wrote: "Federal water rights are entitled to a form of protection that is broader than what may be provided to similarly situated state law rights holders." This flies in the face of state rights and long standing water law across the United States dating back to pre-Constitution in the East and pre-statehood in the West. The Department of Interior, with other agencies are now restricting Tombstone, Arizona's access to and repair of collection systems of Tombstone's adjudicated water rights located on Federal lands. It is doing the same to Arizona ranchers, telling them that they may only access the pipelines and collections points of the ranchers' own water rights if the ranch turns those rights over to the Feds.

Hungry? Tighten Your Belt

A plethora of regulations governing the cultivation of food have tumbled from the computers of Washington bureaucrats who have never held a shovel. Regulations have become political and ideological. Remember the shutdown of a substantial portion of the fertile San Joaquin Valley brought to your attention earlier, or the new farm dust rules. There is a worrisome correlation at all levels of government between new regulations and restrictions, and the overriding theme of Agenda 21, and its spawn of like "policy" documents in the United States.

What's Mine Is Mine and What's Yours Is Mine

Virtually everyone has heard tales or read news accounts of eminent domain run amok. Eminent Domain is the so-called right of a governmental jurisdiction to take or seize private property, if the seizure is deemed to be in the immediate public interest. Owners are many times paid only pennies on the dollar after an arduous and convoluted valuation process. A landmark Supreme Court case that arose from an eminent domain taking in New Haven, Connecticut was unfortunately decided against the landowner by the Supreme Court several years ago. Now, local governments, and a number of states, desperate for money and in ploys to increase their real estate and sales tax base, have seized or attempted to seize entire neighborhoods and blocks only to turn around and give them to a private party planning to build a shopping center or other commercial enterprise.

In the West, eminent domain battles have flared in a number of states as alternative energy projects, both wind and solar, (all of them fueled by 60 to 80% federal subsidies), most of them ill-conceived, premature, and far from any metropolitan area needing the power source, condemned lands for the construction of massive transmission lines through pristine wild lands, some with vertical towers rising one hundred eighty feet (eighteen stories) and placed every thirteen hundred feet, with a road to every tower. It is difficult to comprehend how the earth can be saved by ruining the land.

Some states provide for a payment to a landowner in such cases, not only on the property being taken (the one hundred to three hundred foot easement, times its length across the property,) but also for the diminution of value to the rest the property. Monstrous power lines across your property will detract from value.

Other states have somewhat antiquated laws. Provision for payment of diminution does not exist in the statutes. If a swath across your property is condemned, you will be paid the miniscule amount for the taking, but not the hundreds of thousands, or millions of dollars in value that you will lose. Tough luck.

This is a continually evolving and critical area of law—the sharp edge of property rights, versus government power. I will be updating you in Volume Two and Three on these rapidly developing circumstances. Suffice it to say, when you purchase your land, one of your due diligence checklist items should be the possibility of all, or portion of the land, being subject to some type of eminent domain action—for a power line, a roadway, rapid transit, (a huge problem in Maryland), or other use that some government bureaucrat will subjectively determine to be immediately critical to public welfare. In Volume Two we will discuss how to shut down these types of attempted takings. It is difficult, but it is possible. And in fact, we have done it.

A Maze of Restrictions Flow from Many Levels

Cumbersome and outrageous restrictions unfortunately do not flow just from Washington. Some states, most notably New York, California, Oregon, and Washington, have gone overboard on environmental and land-use restrictions. There are also cities and towns taking steps to exercise greater, and increasingly unrealistic subjective control over your property—New York, San Francisco, Boulder County, CO, Amherst, MA and many other locations. It is important to check state and local laws, while you are putting together your long-term property plan prior to purchasing your property. Understand what you're allowed to do—or more frequently, not allowed to do.

Some states like Colorado will allow you to create a subdivision by merely filing a survey so long as the tracts surveyed are thirty five acres or more. The same used to be true in Montana, but that minimum was increased in the early 1990s to one hundred sixty acres. Wyoming just raised its minimum to one hundred forty acres. Some states don't allow such "survey plats." In those locations, no matter what you want to do with your land, even if it's shave off two hundred acres of your six-hundred-acre parcel, or give an acre to your kids to build their home on the edge of your five-acre parcel, all the planning, zoning and approval steps must be followed to create the tract and allow for its legal transfer. Still other states, notably most of the agricultural states, have some type of provision, (with limitations) whereby you can transfer one, five, or ten acres to a family member (if your operation is agricultural) with minimal paperwork, for the construction of their residence.

We previously discussed mortgage exemptions. A mortgage exemption is a survey done just for financing purposes and is a critical tool in the current regulatory environment because there are limitations on how many acres you can have in your house mortgage. A mortgage exemption survey will create a non-transferable chunk of land that corresponds to the maximum acreage limitation in the new regulatory guidelines, and avoids a costly planning process.

And Then There's the Private

There is a growing trend toward rural acreage Homeowner, Neighborhood or Recreational Ranch Associations. Gated acreage and equestrian communities, and large properties with expansive ranch, farm or wild common areas, surrounded by acreage tracts have become more popular. The covenants for these types of land micro-manage, sometimes down to the color and shapes of mail boxes. Read the Covenants, Architectural Control, By Laws, and other Association documents carefully! Some restrictions are good neighbor common sense and safeguard everyone's values. Others not so much. An effective rule of thumb is, "which restriction that I don't care for, would I be willing to remove from my neighbor's property?" That exercise quickly inserts realistic perspective.

Chapter Thirteen
Finance in the Age of Fiscal Free Fall: The Silver Lining

Yes, conventional financing for land is currently problematic. Regulations of every type and nature are ever constricting. But the essence of land, its soothing balm to your heart, protection for your wallet, and the wide range of goals and objectives land ownership can achieve for you and your family, have not changed. In fact, in my opinion, the current macroeconomic brouhaha has merely heightened the importance and benefits of owning your chunk of earth.

Fortunately, in adversity there is always opportunity. The last time I saw land prices this low on a relative basis was 1979 through 1982, Jimmy Carter's last year, and the first several years of the Reagan presidency. The situation then has many similarities to today's environment—although there are some differences that have evolved with the passage of time.

There are always sellers who want or need to sell. This chapter offers some helpful insights for those of you who fall into in that category. For purchasers, or would-be purchasers of land, my opinion is that there's never been a better time to buy than in the last three decades. Most types of land (other than residential, standard subdivision building lots) have held price levels far better than housing, and certain types of land with production potential are actually increasing in value.

Land prices—other than production ground—remain depressed from their 2005–2007 highs in most areas. Over the last few years though I have not personally purchased, I have assisted others in the buying process, so my opinion is based on sitting in both seats. Some of the outfits with which I'm associated have land for sale. I have the unique insight that flows from talking to many potential buyers and realtors. Over the last six months the number of inquiries has increased, the quality (financial wherewithal of those inquiring) has strengthened, and on a market wide basis there are more contracts and deals in most locations than at any time in the last three years. While housing has not yet bottomed out in most markets based on facts, figures, statistics and languishing prices, I believe—barring unforeseen macroeconomic cataclysm (which might be exactly the time to already own a piece of land and be self-sufficient), the land market appears to be moving upwards from its bottom.

In my mind, there are two basic types of real estate. I call them duplicable real estate, and one-of-a-kind real estate. Here is the way I view this foundational reality:

Anything that can be built—an office building, shopping center, residence—can be duplicated. Someone can always build another. But man cannot create a hill, a view, a river, a vista. Land is one-of-a-kind. There is less and less of it available.

More and more over the past ten years, I've seen folks buying for the long-term—not just their lifetime, but for their family legacy. That land is probably off the market for decades, if not longer. Increasing regulations has removed certain parcels from the mainstream market. Who wants to buy a problem? The ten thousand people a day joining the ranks of retired baby boomers have added additional pressure on the finite supply of land. This group is increasingly active in their search for land. They are looking for investment, retirement, retreat, a safety net, recreation, an inflation hedge, or to return to their roots, which in the case of many baby boomers is a rural or agrarian childhood.

I consider all of these silver linings. These are the foundations of a strengthening market with pent-up and increasing demand. The greatest silver lining, however—besides great prices on a relative basis—is that this is the perfect opportunity for creative financing between a buyer and seller. Referred to as "seller financing," it comes in many forms. It can be via a note and mortgage, a note and deed of trust, or what is known as a contract for deed, which has several variations. There are also options or leases with a right to purchase, along with other mechanisms for specialized situations. Those will be discussed in Volume Two.

Be Imaginative—Be Creative—Be Smart

The truly great thing about a buyer and seller negotiating their own financial structure is that it usually cuts out the time, angst, cost, and potential disappointment of the myriad of hoops thatone must jump through for conventional bank or lender financing. While a buyer is certainly free to get an appraisal prior to purchase, an appraisal is no longer necessary to the deal. The three inch thick pile of documents attendant to a closing with a financial institution is decreased to a fraction of that. Buyers and sellers can negotiate terms and conditions that really suit each of their individual needs, time frames, and cash flows, rather than being restricted to a fairly finite box of "what can and can't be done" in conventional finance. There are no LTV guidelines other than what the seller feels comfortable with taking as a down payment. In a mutually satisfactory seller-financed transaction, it is important that each understand the needs and wants—at least on a general basis—of the other.

Get Assistance

I strongly recommend, in a transaction involving seller financing, regardless of what form of the basic types or iterations referenced above, that each side have a competent local attorney familiar with this aspect of real estate business. A discussion with your CPA regarding the tax impact is certainly warranted. There are some details that need to be thought out and agreed upon that can affect gain, ownership, success, and tax of each of the parties. See the discussion on those matters in Chapter 14.

Sellers!—The Sale Price Doesn't Matter

Do I have your attention? Sellers, remember the "pig is fat and happy rule." In truth, the sale price does not matter. Think about the examples I gave you to ponder in Chapter 11. In both cases, our imaginary seller selling the small piece of property, and our true story seller selling the enormous ranch, less fixation on the sale price, and more time spent noodling the numbers—all the numbers—would lead our imaginary seller in that example to take the deal, and our real-life seller, who's been sitting on his ranch for more than three years, to also sign on the dotted line—at least in my opinion. If I had been a seller in that situation, all things being equal, my response would have been, "Hand me the pen." The only thing that should matter to a seller is what's in my pocket at the end of the transaction. As those examples indicate, computations include inflation rate, carry, operating expense, realistic market trends, personal considerations, and the opportunity cost of money. Factor in the math, and you might accept a deal which you wrinkled your nose at on face value.

Each of the volumes of *Land for Love and Money* will go over these and other points again in different context—they are that important. They need to be repeated. It is natural human propensity to follow form over function when it comes to money. I've done it myself, in several cases much to my regret. The workbook for Volume One will contain actual contract clauses and deal structures that can be employed, or mutated and employed, to fit a particular situation (after thorough review by your team!).

Never forget, every real estate transaction is absolutely unique from every other real estate transaction, ever. It's like that snapshot you take of the setting sun at 6:02 PM on April 17, 2012: crimson tendrils of clouds fading into indigo as the great yellow orb descends below the horizon. That scene will never be repeated. That second will never again exist exactly as it exists at that moment. This is true for real estate transactions. Every buyer is completely unique. Every seller is completely unique. The situations of each are fluid. Every property is completely unique. The nexus of those elements means that every transaction is different in both small and material respects from every other transaction, even if on the same land. Here are some bullet points, which in my experience are universal in their application to sellers:

1) Sale price is not important. What's in your pocket at the end of the day, after tax and all expenses, is what matters.

2) In almost all instances a bird in the hand is worth two in the

bush. If you're lucky enough to have multiple buyers looking at the property, there are things you and your advisors can do to buy time to get as many offers and the highest contract amount possible. However, if it comes down to maybe getting some more money from "buyer number two," who is maybe going to submit a contract, that maybe might have the terms and conditions you are looking for, as opposed to signing the contract in hand from "buyer number one" (assuming the buyers are equal in capability), putting your John Henry on the dotted line of the contract in hand is the wisest course of action.

3) While perhaps true in the go-go days of the hot markets, the assumption that there's another buyer, and he will be eagerly striding in your door with a wide smile, contract and check in hand if you don't take the deal on the table, is not a great assumption in the current environment. Remember our ranch seller in Chapter 11.

4) In today's volatile world things can change in a second, without warning. Regulations at the state, federal, or local level might materialize and preclude or delay the sale you put off. Macroeconomic or world events, or elections, can frighten buyers, make them pull in their horns, invoke a contingency in the purchase agreement and get their earnest money back. If you are a seller, time is not your ally.

5) Do not rely on the fact that your bank will work with you on financing extensions or modifications in the current climate. They may want to, but their hands could be tied by regulators.

In the worst case, your bank might fail in the lapse of time, in which case any latitude you've been counting on in dealing with your property, sale, or some modification of your note will vanish. An acquiring bank frankly doesn't care about you, your property, the market, the deal, the taxpayers or the buyer. They want their guaranteed profit from the Loss Share Agreement.

6) No one is going to buy your property without seeing it. No one's going to bother to come look at it if the price is too high in the multiple listing service in which your broker has it displayed, or in the for sale by owner (FSBO) marketing you are conducting if trying to sell it yourself. Market your property to get a buyer's boots on the ground. That means realistic pricing. If you ascribe a pie-in-the-sky value you are wasting marketing money and time, and perhaps dissuading a buyer who would otherwise have toured the dirt and bought it.

7) Whether or not you are represented by a realtor, preassemble a good team. Have the packages for the property in their files—maps, plat, listing agreement, old appraisals if you have one, copies of any leases or agreements that affect the property, a title report with a copy of the title exceptions, tax, revenue and expense statements, and water or other rights. This way your team is in the know, they can hit the ground running and advise you intelligently when you're negotiating an offer.

8) Understand your tax situation. There are several gotchas in this regard. A portion of your property may have been depreciated. You will not get capital gains on any portion of the transaction

having to do with those types of assets. This is discussed more fully in Chapter 14. Your CPA can tell you the adjusted cost basis in your land and real estate. In the most simplistic terms, this is what you bought it for, less certain transactions which may reduce cost, plus money you've put into improvements. That sum (there are other ingredients) is your cost. The amount over that cost will be taxable gain of several varieties.

Buyer Considerations

There is some surprising overlap between the needs, wants and goals of both the buyer and the seller. But there are certainly positions unique to a buyer and contrary to what might be best for seller. Welcome to the free market. These matters are also discussed more fully in Chapter 14. But here are some bullet point universal truths that I employ, and which I believe a buyer should keep in mind when looking for, investigating, and purchasing a piece of land or real estate:

1) I believe the seller is entitled to either price or terms. Softer terms affords you latitude to pay a higher price. Stiff terms—such as all-cash, should result in a price discount.

2) The cleaner your offer, the more likely you are to get the structural or financial goodies you really want. Sometimes complex offers are unavoidable because the property, or the seller and buyer situations, are complicated. But generally speaking, clean is good. Keep your contingencies to a minimum. If there are some glaring potential problems, consult with your realtor and attorney and perhaps you will want to list them. I prefer

simply to list one overriding contingency as a buyer: *"After or during buyer's investigation of the property, if Buyer determines in his absolute and sole discretion that the property, or any portion or aspect thereof, will not work for his intended use of or plan for the property, Buyer may terminate this Agreement by written notice to Seller, and all monies paid, including earnest money, shall be returned to Buyer and neither party shall have any further liability or obligation to the other."* That can save pages. And let's face it—everybody gets it. Basically, "if I don't like your property for any reason I am not going to buy it, and I get my money back."

3) The "PPPPP" rule. Have a plan put together for this property before the expiration of the contingency period in the contract. It can be rough, it will certainly change, but it is important for you to understand generally at least what you can and want to do with the property, what your goals are, what steps you need to take to achieve those objectives, what the potential results are, and when they are likely to occur.

4) This point will have to be negotiated between you and the buyer. I highly recommend exculpatory language in the seller financing documents. This means that the seller is looking to the property, and not to you, if things go bad in the future. I think it's fair in those instances for you to potentially be liable (if your attorney agrees) for any alterations you make to the property that would be adverse to future value as determined by an independent appraiser.

5) Decide which form of financial contract works best for you.

Laws vary state to state concerning mortgages, deeds of trust, and contracts for deed. You must have a local attorney assist you in these matters. Your realtor is not allowed to. Your CPA is not a lawyer. Do not use a lawyer in Florida to draft a purchase and sale agreement for a deal in Minnesota.

6) When you solidify the financial structure of your offer, how much down, when you want to make payments, if you want to make principal payments or just interest, if the finance will be amortized or not, when the payoff of whatever balance remains will be due, you need to mix the reality of your financial situation with pessimistic assumptions about your future income. These are not realistic assumptions, or optimistic assumptions, but instead your projections should be based on the maxim that what can go wrong will go wrong. Just look at the last four years. Did you expect the wreck when you did deals (whether real estate or otherwise) in 2005, 2006 and 2007? Probably not.

7) Base your offer, down payment, and the cash going out of your pocket to carry the property on this realistic worst-case assumption. As the *Green for Green* workbook will demonstrate, there are many ways for you to pay down the obligation, reduce interest carry, or prepay, with prepayments lowering future payments at your discretion. This might benefit you if rainy days come later.

8) Do not skimp on your due diligence. Turn over those rocks. The larger and more complex the property the longer you need to do a thorough job. Be sure you personally inspect the land

and property. Be sure you get copies of any of the documents referenced as exceptions in the title report. Take the time to understand your tax situation, at least projected, over the course of ownership and in the event of disposition, even if your plan is to not sell the property. If you have plans for improvements on the property, intend to transfer portions of it, contemplate future conservation easements, absolutely talk to potential Grantees for the conservation easements, local jurisdictions which will be issuing permits for the improvements, reputable contractors if the plan includes building structures, and neighboring landowners if you're planning improvements to increase or begin agricultural and livestock production.

The above is not exhaustive, but is intended to be universal. There will be peculiarities to locations, climate, local and state statures. Whether you are selling or buying, and regardless of size or dollar amount, this transaction is significant on both a financial and personal level. Give it the care, attention, energy and time it deserves.

Chapter Fourteen
When Love and Money Collide
The Purchase: Buying Smart—
The Devil Is in the Details

I'm often asked to describe the "perfect" buyer/seller transaction. My first response, with a wide grin, is always "all cash–no contingencies." However, no deal is ever like another one, which makes the query difficult to realistically answer. Given today's economic conditions and high likelihood of seller finance, a buy/sell which would tickle me on a personal and financial level would be something similar to this:

A Deal Made in Heaven

Let's start with the nonfinancial aspects.

- There has to be at least a modicum of trust between a buyer and the seller. It's helpful if there is a point or two of commonality. Perhaps they share the same interests. Maybe they're both ranchers, horsemen, love the beach, are avid hunters, like to fish, or are the same age—some type of common ground is always helpful.
- The transaction should be one in which neither the buyer nor seller is under any duress, that is they must buy or sell. A deal is usually far more smooth and enjoyable if neither of the parties is in a position of having to sign, "or else."
- A real estate contract and closing breeds a myriad of details

> and entails a large cast of characters. Each party needs to rely on the other. Each needs to have faith in the members of the opposite team to do what they say, when they say they're going to do it. And, if a problem arises, both parties need to feel secure in the belief that they will hear about it immediately, and everyone will work in good faith toward a mutually beneficial solution.

Assuming you have that type of relationship with the folks on the other side of the table, you have the foundation for a satisfying high-energy process. Mutual respect will positively lead to a smoother closing.

A Note of Caution—Always Trust Your Gut

Unfortunately, not everyone is honest and there are some folks who excel at putting on a charade. No matter how strong your comfort level is with the people on the other side of the transaction, keep your antennae in the air. Sometimes things are not what you think, or what they appear to be. Reality can be different than what others would have you believe. If, in the breeze of purchase or sale, any red flags run up the flagpole, heed the warning snap of that pennant. Later in this chapter there is a remarkable example of why I inject this note of caution.

The Perfect Deal

There is, of course, no such thing as the "perfect deal." A great deal is when everybody is happy, leaves the closing table with a smile, and wishes they could have gotten a little bit more in this clause or that, but are generally well satisfied. That's a deal likely to last and be honored over the years. Remember, in a seller financed transaction, the buyer's and seller's interaction does not end when you shake hands after the closing. If you are the buyer, you owe money, and if you are seller, you are owed money. The two of you will be doing business for quite some time. All things being equal, the structure of the "perfect deal" (seller financed) would include the following:

1) Some continuing responsibility by the seller after closing in certain key areas, for instance environmental hazards. I will not purchase property when the seller refuses to represent that there are no environmental problems, and warrant that such representations are correct and agrees that those warranties extend forever past closing, which must be specified. Without a so called "anti-merger clause" any such warranties, along with all others, will merge with closing and be extinguished.

2) The financial structure of the deal keeps the buyer cash down payment to a reasonable minimum, perhaps between 15% and 25%. There are incentives built into the documents for the buyer to pay faster and earlier than the dates in the agreements. For instance, (and these unique clauses of ours will be included in the *Green for Green* workbook), the buyer has a right to prepay the amount he owes seller at any time without penalty. If the buyer does prepay, the buyer has the right to subtract those prepayments from future principal and interest payments due under the financing instruments. If John the buyer owes $20,000 each December, and one year he pays $40,000, he can elect to subtract the extra $20,000 he paid early from some future payment. That clause can come in handy during unexpected periods of tight cash flow.

3) If a buyer has plans to improve the property, those improvements typically enhance the value of the seller's property, which is the collateral. As a buyer, I want as much cash available as possible to make the improvements and increase the value of the property. As a seller, I'm smiling whenever the buyer spends his money on the land I have as security. In effect, he's added value and lowered my LTV (loan to value).

4) Unforeseen events occur. Life happens. A clause in a seller financing instrument, which allows a buyer to make partial releases from the seller's security interest for the payment of a set amount (agreed upfront in the financing documents), which can be per acre or otherwise, is a good idea. It can save the day for both buyer and seller if events occur outside their control. Protections for the seller are needed for the release clause to be fair. He doesn't want the rest of his property inaccessible because some third party bought the road. He doesn't want his property checker-boarded, which would decrease its value and be a nightmare if he ever had to take it back. Release clauses that mandate releases be contiguous to an outer boundary, or contiguous to a previous release, and cannot restrict access to the balance of the property on which the buyer still owes money, are fair. These provisions benefit both parties and usually will get more cash to the seller in a shorter time frame.

5) The grant of a conservation easement is not effective unless there is subordination by the lender. The easement is a grant in perpetuity, i.e., forever. Therefore it can't be in a position to get foreclosed out by a lien prior in title. When a foreclosure occurs, everything behind that foreclosed lien is wiped out. Whether

or not conservation easements or similar devices are part of the buyer's plan, it behooves both parties to make allowances for that possibility up front. It is fair for a seller to subordinate to the grant of an easement, but it is also equitable that the seller be protected. The seller should not have to subordinate to an easement that strips all rights to the property. He's getting no tax benefit. If he ever has to take the property back, he certainly doesn't want land he cannot resell. By subordinating, the seller is taking on some risk. It's fair that people be compensated for risk. Perhaps a per acre amount as a subordination fee (which would apply to the note and could even be a prepayment), could be agreed upon up front.

6) The seller generally certifies that all things of value and all rights appurtenant to the property such as water rights, mineral rights, easement interests, etc., have been delivered to the buyer. Sometimes quite unintentionally, rights are discovered after the fact. The seller's obligation to promptly transfer those to the buyer is a provision that should survive closing.

7) Sometimes people get into disagreements. There should be provisions in the documents that require written notice be given by one party to the other long in advance of filing a lawsuit or taking other adversarial action. This way the party who has received a notice has time to correct the problem if it exists, and there's an opportunity for buyer and seller, or their representatives, to resolve the matter before it becomes an expensive mess.

8) The parties should agree up front what types of improvements the buyer cannot make without asking the seller's permission.

Most improvements should not warrant any further future interaction. It is far simpler to do the short list of "not allowed" rather than the far more lengthy compilation of what is "ok." However, if there is an extraordinary undertaking then the purchaser has to request permission from the seller before undertaking the work.

For example, let's say Sally is buying twenty acres from Roger. She wants to fence the twenty acres for horses, develop a spring into a small pond, remodel the house, build a barn, put in an arched entryway and similar types of improvements. These are great for both parties. Sally adds value to the property she is purchasing and enjoys that spiritual lift that always comes with giving TLC to your piece of heaven. Roger is thrilled because the value of the property he holds as collateral is escalating—it's all Sally's money, and with each improvement his loan position becomes more secure. Now, say five acres of this hypothetical twenty-acre place is in hay production. Sally decides that it would be a terrific investment to take it out of hay and instead, begin a Christmas tree farm. In this case, Roger should have the right to say no. Roger may not want the hay base taken out. This type of improvement could change the nature of the property. If he has to take the property back, he may not want to be watering all those evergreen saplings for the three to six years it takes them to become salable Christmas trees.

9) Another great way to avoid disputes is to determine potential problem areas between the buyer and seller in advance. If future valuations are required, disputes can arise as to who is the proper appraiser. The easy way to fix this is ensure the documents

specify that each of the parties can select an appraiser and those two appraisers will pick a third appraiser. That selection and the appraisal are binding. This type of strategy will work in virtually every instance where there might be a suspicion by either party that a consultant, appraiser, or other third-party has loyalties that lean one way or the other.

I have found it worthwhile to take some time before the closing, think about what could go wrong in the future and how those problems, if they ever arise, can be solved without litigation.

When Love and Money Collide—The Purchase

It's the day of closing. If you're the seller, you're excited. You're getting a check and moving the asset. That ebullience may be tinged with some remorse if it's a piece of land you truly loved, or that ties in with family or other memories. If you're the buyer, you're about to realize a dream and are filled with enthusiasm, imagining the enjoyment of your acquisition, making improvements, and finding satisfaction in its operation.

The Labyrinth of the Closing

If you've done your homework and followed the "PPPPP" rule, there will be few, if any, surprises at the closing table. If you have not, a closing can be gruesome. I've seen many cases where shortly before closing a seller has tried to skate, twist, or completely crawfish out of the purchase and sale agreement. Perhaps somebody has approached and offered him more money. Perhaps some pressure has arisen that is clouding his judgment. I've seen the same thing happen on the buyer side. The buyer has suffered some type of financial reversal he didn't count on. Maybe in the course of his wanderings between the time of the contract and the closing he found another property, which he thinks is a better deal. Desperate people do desperate things.

Sometimes one or the other of the parties just gets greedy, or they believe they have some leverage to press for last-minute concessions. These types of situations cause rancor, especially in cases where the party who's planning to stick with the deal honestly thought there was some camaraderie and mutual respect. The shock of being wrong in your judgment about the human on the other side of the contract coupled with the unpleasant effect to your business plan causes anger that somebody is trying to change the deal, and can make for an unpleasant experience and leave a bitter taste.

In some cases the party who's willing to stick with the deal has decisions to make. Should he/she accede to the demands of the other party? Partially accede (work out a compromise and get it done even though it is not the original deal)? Walk away from the deal and begin the arduous process all over, leaving time, effort, energy, hope and funds expended for legal and other costs on the table? Or, dig in his/her heels based on principle and business, and hold the feet of the flaky party to the fire of the agreement.

*****

Twenty years ago, a group that I was representing and later became a partner in, made an offer on an exquisite ranch on one of the major rivers in Montana. After a month of negotiations, the purchase and sale agreement was signed. They were excited, had made their plans, had invested considerable funds in due diligence and had even begun the permit process for several improvements they planned to commence immediately after closing. This was a seller financed transaction. The sellers were extremely wealthy, lived elsewhere and spent little time on this wonderful property. As part of the deal, the buyers were required to furnish the sellers their financial statements. The sellers had the right to approve or disapprove. If they disapproved, the deal was over.

Within a few days of execution of the contract, the buyers submitted their financial statements– which I will disclose were extremely impressive, and demonstrated financial capabilities that could have purchased a property fifty times the size of the one on the table. There were no objections by the seller.

Four days before closing, almost three months after the contract was signed and financial statements had been submitted, we received an out-of-the-blue e-mail from the seller's attorney stating that the sellers disapproved the buyer's balance sheet and were canceling the contract.

I knew from my upfront work for the buyers that this was an exceptional deal. The minute I was informed of the sudden, suspicious shift, and unwarranted last minute attempted termination of contract, I knew that the sellers had received another offer for more money.

My buyers were distraught. Some of the group wanted to say "the hell with it." Others wanted to force the issue. I recommended that they force the issue. A Lis Pendens was filed on the property, which means it could not be transferred to anyone else until a court decided who was right and wrong. My clients filed a complaint to enforce the specific performance[1] provisions of the purchase and sale agreement.

In the meantime, I went to work via the sagebrush grapevine

to gather what intelligence I could about what was really going on. My suspicions were confirmed. The sellers had indeed received a higher offer. To make matters worse they had deliberately tried to conceal it from my buyers. Several months of wrangling elapsed. In the court process, the sellers learned that the buyers knew exactly what happened, and the matter was settled shortly thereafter. Not only did my buyers get the ranch pursuant to the contract that had originally been signed, but the sellers reduced the price $100,000 as settlement of the legal action.

There are countless details in real estate. They are unavoidable. Real estate and land are multifaceted assets. I have seen, though not often, closings deteriorate into frigid silences, flushed faces and clenched jaws just because of a detail—though insignificant in the general exponentially larger scheme of the transaction—was not thought of and provided for up front.

Some of the gotchas in this category could be:

Who gets the propane and the propane tank. Many rural properties rely on a propane energy source. Generally tanks are five hundred or one thousand gallons. At $2-plus plus a gallon, a thousand gallon tank represents $2,000. A seller's realtor should be sure the sellers are protected, the fill level of the propane tank is checked the day before closing, and the seller is paid by the buyer at closing for the propane still left in the tank. You'd be amazed at how often this detail is overlooked and astounded at the arguments that can erupt at the closing table even while consummating seven-figure transactions.

Insurance is another important detail and potential problem

[1]A remedy available to buyers and sellers if in the contract which allows the non-defaulting party to force the other party to "specifically perform," i.e., complete the transaction pursuant to the contract, and pay the legal fees of both sides.

area. If the sellers are carrying money for the buyer, obviously the seller needs some protection if the house, barn or other flammable structure burns down or is otherwise destroyed. That's part of the seller's collateral. All sorts of nasty fights can erupt at closing table over whether the seller gets the insurance money in the event of a calamity, or the funds are available to the buyer to rebuild the structure thereby restoring the seller to his original collateral position.

Disputes can arise over the proration of taxes, improvement districts, homeowners association dues, the electric bill in the month of closing, assessments on water rights, the split of crops or pasture in an ongoing operation. The list is endless. There will be a helpful closing checklist in the *Green for Green* workbook.

The lesson here is that a layman, not involved in the real estate business, is simply not going to know about all these details. But your advisory team should. Far better to leave the closing table with a grin and a handshake then a grimace and a mutter. Then there are the frauds—despicable, distasteful and incredible.

What They Knew but Didn't Tell You

The first rule of real estate is disclosure. It's mandated by both law and ethics if you are a real estate professional, realtor or attorney. It's also required that the seller disclose any material adverse facts he knows related to the property he is selling. Sometimes an untruth, or purposeful omission is caught during the due diligence process buried in the paperwork. Ten years ago a group with which I was involved was purchasing a small ranch. The ranch house was fed by a well. The sellers represented it was a "good, deep well" that had a flow of twenty gallons a minute.

When I'm acting as a fiduciary for partners I trust the seller, but in the wise words of Ronald Reagan, I verify. I had the hydrology consultant who was checking some other aspects of the ranch, also run a test on the well. The "good, deep well" turned out to be twenty-two feet deep, with a nine parts-per-million E. coli bacteria level (bring your hazmat suit!), and a flow rate of under six gallons a minute. Worse yet, we discovered the seller had had the well tested several years prior and knew about the problems.

* * * * *

One particular attempted fraud always sticks in my mind. This was another rare occasion in which I was representing a third party buyer purchasing a smaller horse property. (I keep giving examples of these "rare" occasions—but when you have been involved in 5,000+ transactions and have acted as buyer's agent perhaps one hundred times, they are "rare"—all things are relative). There were two other realtors involved in this transaction.

My clients and I had met the sellers and their agent on the first inspection of the property, which was a twenty-two-acre small rolling farm property beautifully located near water, secluded, with a very fine home. My buyers really liked the sellers, and the seller's realtor. I liked the seller's realtor though I knew she was far sharper than her cloak of good ol' girl demeanor. I liked the wife of the seller. However, there was some current of energy when I met the husband that I couldn't quite place, but it made me uneasy and put me on guard. My clients pooh-poohed my disclosure of that impression after we left the property.

The clients had looked at several other properties, decided that this twenty-two-acre spread was perfect and wanted to submit an offer. Because everybody seemed to get along so well, we all agreed to meet in their kitchen and see if we couldn't verbally cut a deal that would then be transferred to a purchase and sale agreement. For a while, the meeting was as cordial as a negotiating session can be.

The husband then began to explain that they had planned to build a metal barn, the contracts had already been signed with a contractor, they had paid a deposit, the contract could not be cancelled, and work was supposed to start shortly. They could not sell the property unless my client agreed to follow through on the contract and build the structure as designed, and pay for the costs of construction. This was a significant unexpected wrinkle, and strange. Why would a seller force a buyer to construct any building (much less, in my opinion, an unattractive metal box located in the wrong place on the property)?

The sellers remained in the kitchen while the buyers' group stepped outside to discuss this most unexpected information about the barn. Birds fluttered in the sun-filled afternoon, the water sparkled and geese honked contentedly. I knew that despite my advice, my clients were going to cave in. My clients believed the sellers—that the contract could not be canceled and that they would not sell the property unless the buyer agreed to build the barn.

My antennae were at full alert. There's virtually no construction agreement I have been associated with—and I have been associated with my share—that could not be canceled. Although, in some cases, if materials had been purchased or plans had been drawn, the agreement usually specified a penalty. That's more than fair.

Despite my recommendations and the recommendations of the other realtor on the buyer side of the equation, the buyers decided they would accept the condition. We went back into the kitchen, and I asked what the cost of the barn was. There was a flicker in the husband's eyes—almost imperceptible—but nonetheless real. He said the barn would cost $30,000, but that he would handle everything, the buyers could pay him and he would pay the contractor. He said he had a relationship with the contractor and was familiar with the project. He was "only too happy to assist." My antennae were now buzzing.

I asked to see a copy of the contract. The husband made a great show of rummaging around in desks and looking for the contract he had just expressed such great concern over. In the end he "couldn't find it." He did find one sheet of the contract bearing his signature and that of contractor, but with no other information. I got everyone to agree that within seventy-two hours after both parties executed a purchase agreement, the contract would be supplied and would become an exhibit to the agreement, and that my buyers would have five days to approve that document. The purchase and sale agreement was drawn, greatly complicated with details and clauses to protect both buyer and seller on the future construction project that the seller wanted to supervise for the buyer. The contract was signed.

Four days later I called the selling broker and asked for the barn contract. She hemmed and hawed and said her clients had not yet located it. I suggested that the contractor must have a copy, perhaps they could get it from him. Another week went by and still no contract. By now I was certain that my immediate suspicions when the matter arose in the kitchen were correct. The seller was trying to make additional money on the barn.

I called the contractor direct. He and I got along fine and I asked him what the cost of construction was. He said it wouldn't be more than $30,000, but there was a slight hesitation to his answer. He confirmed he had a copy of the contract, but could not release it without the seller's permission.

I went to my clients and told them my suspicions. Again, they pooh-poohed my misgivings, but gave me the latitude to do what was necessary to confirm or dismiss my suppositions.

I sat down with the selling broker and we had a heart-to-heart. I reminded her that without the referenced exhibit of the construction contract, the purchase and sale agreement was not complete. I told her my clients would take no further steps toward closing nor incur any further due diligence expense until a full and complete exhibit of the construction agreement was provided and attached to the contract as called for in the agreement.

Another week went by. I called the selling broker several times, with no response. Finally, she got back to me with the news that the sellers were going to drop the condition that the barn be built. She hopefully suggested that the need for, and reference to that exhibit, would be removed. The only thing the sellers requested from the buyers was that the buyers pay the 50% of the contract termination fee, which was $1,000. My clients agreed to pay 50% to get rid of the morass and the long-term liability of an ugly barn in the wrong place, but now they were curious, too. I requested that they give me the authority to make their $1,000 contingent upon seeing the construction contract, which had never been furnished.

The look of relief on the selling broker's face when I told her my clients agreed, other than one small request, could not be missed. When I told her the small request was that for the $1,000 they at least wanted to see the contract they were paying to terminate, the look of alarm that flashed across her features was also unmistakable.[2]

The property closed. The sellers never even attended the closing, and finally, a week after closing, the selling broker called me and said she had a copy of the barn construction contract and would trade me for my clients' check.

The contract was for $21,000. This entire drama on an expensive property in a soft market, the associated bad feelings, distrust, abrasion and potential loss of the entire transaction, had been over the seller's attempt to make an extra $9,000, based on a lie.

Let me emphasize that the story I just shared with you is the *exception* rather than the rule. Most sellers, particularly of rural land, are honest and conscientious. In most cases, they love the land they're selling and they want the buyer to love it too—land touches hearts that way.

The conclusion? Pay attention to the details to avoid a wreck. If there's something suspicious, or information doesn't jive, trust your gut and investigate, and if there is a "disturbance in the Force," i.e., the energy of the people on the other side the table changes or turns, there's a reason.

[2]In the selling broker's partial defense, I do not believe she initially knew of the attempted fraud by her clients. However, at some point in the process—perhaps when they abruptly reversed their insistence the barn built, she did.

Chapter Fifteen
Tax with a Twist

The tax laws of the United States are anything but simple. The entire U.S. Tax Code now consists of approximately eighty thousand pages, up from a "mere" sixteen thousand pages, thirty-plus years ago. While tax law is not straight forward for any industry or asset, I believe real estate is among the most complex and most varied. This chapter is not meant to be down in the trenches with references of cites, code sections and tax case results from the tens of thousands of lawsuits that eighty thousand pages has spawned. Rather, it is an overview, a taste of the smorgasbord of potentially advantageous, and possibly disastrous, major real estate related quirks in the Code.[1]

Tax Your Biggest Expense

People complain about the price of gas, the cost of food, housing, college tuitions and a host of other life expenses. But the biggest single expense in life and real estate is tax. One of these days perhaps the Code will be simplified. It could be cut down to under five hundred pages, raise more revenue for the Treasury and unleash the economic power of American industry, workers, real estate and the land's resources. One can only hope.

[1]For url links to Tax Code details, see the Resources section in the back of this volume.

For now, however, it is what it is. As this book goes to press there is political screeching about changes in rates, the expiration of President Bush's Tax Cuts, and a host of other tax variables. This uncertainty is not helpful to the real estate market or to the economy in general. Uncertain people are not great at making decisions. It's a fact of life. In all likelihood, portions of this chapter will be outdated come January 1, 2013. I plan to update these volumes on the *Land for Love and Money* website (www.landforloveandlovemoney.com) according to its terms, and in future printings of these volumes, so that they're always fresh and current, known as "evergreen" in the publishing industry.

If tax is your biggest expense in life and in real estate, it makes sense that you should pay attention to the tax effect of your decisions regarding the likely largest asset in your portfolio, i.e., the real estate you already own, and land and real estate that you plan to purchase or sell. I'm amazed at how few people take into account the dramatic tax whack to their land and real estate oriented revenues. Even at the lowest 15% capital gains rate, the tax that you're paying on your gain is 9% higher than the commission you paid your realtor (assuming you're represented) on that portion of the transaction.

The government is now talking about additional real estate taxes. A hidden 3% tax when you sell real estate that would go to Obamacare, a potential national sales tax on real estate, and a host of other discussions. All these also remain uncertain. Many have been voiced for decades. Other than to make you aware that there are potential additional tax gotchas being discussed for the future, they are not worth your time or mine. More relevant are the basic types of tax paid under current law on real estate, real estate transactions, and real estate income, whether on raw or improved land. If your plan for your property does not integrate tax projections—do a new plan.

I want to emphasize, I'm not a CPA or tax expert. Everyone's tax situation is different just as everyone's real estate is different. Even if your only land and real estate asset is a lot with a house, it is worth a few hours discussion with your CPA or tax preparer to review tax savings you are probably leaving on the table, and the tax effect of decisions you may make in the future.

A Menu of Rates for a Smorgasbord of Matters—Looking at the Big Picture

Capital Gains—The Best

When you sell a property (and if you are not a "dealer"), and you have held the property for at least a year and a day, any profit is called long-term capital gains. The tax rate is 15%. The taxable gain may be more or less than the cash you get at the closing table. If there is taxable gain for which you don't receive cash, it is known as "phantom income." There are other factors such as depreciation, mortgage and similar deductions, certain exclusions as to part of the gain for married couples or single folks if the sale property is your primary residence—up to $250,000 for an individual and $500,000 per couple. A sizable tax savings.

There's Land and Structure—And Other Stuff

All real estate has certain assets other than land or structures which will not last the life of the real estate. They fall into a number of classes. Rather than bog us down with all of them, I will just term this group of real estate related assets "personal property." Personal property can be depreciated. In other words, it has a finite useful life in the eyes of the tax man. Each year it is worth less. The "decrease in remaining useful life" becomes a deduction. Certain types of assets have a three year depreciation life, some five, some seven. The pro-rata annual depreciation that you take as deduction reduces your taxable income.[2]

As an example, let's say you have a $7,000 hot tub. Its useful life is seven years. In the most simplistic terms, your accountant is depreciating that asset $1,000 a year. If you are in a 20% tax bracket, that is saving you $200 in taxes a year. However there's a flipside to the depreciation benefit. When you sell your property, good advisors will segregate capital gains assets from the depreciable assets and they'll be listed separately in the contract. As a seller you always want to keep that number as low as possible. Using our hot tub example if you owned the property for five years before you sold, you've depreciated the hot tub $5,000. If the hot tub in your sale is valued at $5,000, you have a $3,000 phantom income depreciation recapture. You don't get 15% capital gains on that "gain". You pay at the highest ordinary income rate. As a fun aside—if you have a medical condition and a bona-fide certification from a doctor that a hot tub, or similar improvement, is prescribed for that condition—you can deduct its purchase as a medical expense. Ask you CPA!

The larger your piece of land, the more personal assets you might have. Think of gates, fences, entryways, equipment, machinery and sprinklers that "run with" or are sold with the land and a host of other items. I've actually seen real estate transactions where, if you segregated out the tax on the depreciation recapture, it was higher than the capital gains tax on the gain of the property, mostly because

[2]Certain types of property, such as commercial and a narrow band of production property, can depreciate buildings in addition to personal property over 39.5 years. A "segmented cost study" can separate out components (heating system for instance) and those components can be depreciated more quickly.

somebody was lazy, didn't do their homework or take the time to properly assess the personal property part of the transaction. This can mean *significant* dollars out of your pocket.

The buyer wants the highest possible value on personal property. A buyer should list out, or at least aggregate, the legitimate value of personal property as an item separate from the land at the time of purchase. Why? Because the purchase price is what it is. That means the greater the value attributed to personal property the less the value or cost of the land and real estate. When it comes time to sell, less cost in the land and real estate increases capital gain that is taxed at a lower rate. This is another example of the "PPPPP" rule.

Remember that buyers and sellers are working from opposite extremes when it comes to personal property. It will take some negotiation, the final result has to be legitimate and substantiated, but in over forty years of real estate I've never seen a deal lost over the valuation of personal property.

If the Feds Don't Get You, the Locals Will—Cash Flow Is as Much Savings as Income!

Real estate carries with it an ugly fact of life. Property taxes. Property taxes in some locations can be astronomical. A $1 million property in Connecticut on several acres could easily be paying (particularly in the southern part of the state), $30,000 or more in property taxes per year. That same property, if you could pull a Harry Potter and apparate it to a more remote region in the Midwest or the Rockies, would be subject to property tax—depending on location—of under $5,000. If the property has acreage enough to generate minimum agricultural income, usually about $1,500 year (though that can vary from locality to locality) it can qualify for

Agricultural Exemption, and that $5,000 tax bill will be less than $2,000+/- year.

Remember our discussion about investigations into the *area* in which you want to purchase property? Add property taxes to your list of what to check out. Property taxes are an income mainstay of municipal governments that are mostly starved for cash. They're based on the localities' appraisal—called an assessment—of the value of your property, times a rate that is called the millage or mill rate. I'm going to resist the temptation to eat up many pages on this topic. Suffice it to say that the higher the assessment, and the higher the mill rate, the more tax you pay. Your property taxes go to municipal administration, municipal services, schools and a host of other services. More and more of your money is also going to bloated pension obligations—paying the costs of workers who are no longer even in "your employ."

An extra bit of land and a little effort to create bona-fide income from that land can save you a multiple of the actual income in property taxes. A check you don't write is a check you receive. The old colloquialism "a penny saved is a penny earned" applies. Savings on property taxes is like getting a check. Improvements like fencing to create or enhance pasture, starting a commercial vegetable garden, feeding the neighbor's horse, can create a level of income qualifying you for the exemptions. Your land, no matter how small the tract, is beginning to work for you—generating and/or saving significant cash flows.

Dealer Status—Not a Good Thing

People who "flip" multiple properties in short terms (under one year) as their livelihood, hold properties for less than a year, sell multiples of lots as a developer, or homes as a builder are regarded as "dealers" by the Service. Cash-strapped state governments have lately been trying illegitimately and mostly unsuccessfully to tag others who are in no way dealers with "dealer status" because like the Feds, the state gets higher tax revenues from a dealer transaction than from a capital gains transaction. Some startling stories on that in Volume Two.

Talk to your CPA and attorney if you're involved with more than one piece of real estate so that you never have to defend against a governmental claim, no matter how bogus, that you are a dealer.

Work the Land—Make the Land Your Partner

Work the tax angle of your real estate. Ask your CPA what tax benefits your real estate can generate for you. If you have a home office in the ranch or farm house, or any residential structure, it can save you tax. If your home office is two hundred square feet, and your home is two thousand square feet, very simply speaking, you can get certain benefits on 10% of your home expenses.

Thinking of putting in an improvement? Check its depreciable life. Not all, but a portion of the improvement can be paid for over time with depreciation tax benefits. But, remember the recapture.

If you have several acres or more you can form a LLC or S-Corp. and put a portion of the land under its name. Be sure this is not a default under your mortgage or any other document or covenant on the land. If your entity is *legitimately* "for profit", trying to make income and profit off the land through pasture, crops, etc, then there are expenses that you can write off via the LLC related to those efforts that you could not take as simply residential. This can be far more advantageous than merely allowing the acres to sit there as residential. Review your plan with your CPA! Basically, you've taken a portion of a personal asset, and converted it to a business asset. There are benefits to business assets and running a business. Besides money, there's a love thing going on here, too!

Land that you care for, improve, become involved with, nurture and put to work for you, becomes a part of you, creates a bond, a mingling of energy, and for most people a deep sense of satisfaction.

Your own vegetables always taste best!

Tax with a Twist

There are bewildering assortments of provisions in the Code that allow you to shelter gain when you sell a property at a profit. These are tactical, advanced, and complicated. Always employ a competent attorney and CPA when employing these mechanisms.

The "Easy" One—The 1031[3]

The first is what's known as a 1031 tax-deferred exchange. The seller takes all or part of the gain from the sale of one property and invests it into the purchase of a similar "like kind"[4] property. Whatever amount of the gain you invest in the new property is not taxable, that is until eventually the property is sold and you don't buy another. Then tax is owed on the 1031 gain or gains that were previously deferred. Note this—your personal residence will *not* qualify for 1031 treatment.

When writing a real estate purchase offer or sales contract, even if neither party contemplates a 1031 exchange or other tax-deferred mechanism, it's worthwhile to provide in the contract that either party may invoke a tax-deferral strategy so long as that election is at

[3]See Resources section for url links.
[4]In very simple terms (check specifics with your CPA) land for land, house for house, commercial property to commercial property.

no cost to the other party. Life happens. "PPPPP". Is it worth taking one minute to add a paragraph of boilerplate language beneficial to buyer and seller (even if its use is not contemplated), for a potential tax savings in the thousands, hundreds of thousands or even millions of dollars on a large property? You bet it is. "PPPPP".

The Facilitator Is Your Friend

An integral part of a 1031 and other similar types of exchanges is the exchange agent, also known as the facilitator. They handle all the documents. They take title to the exchange property, even if it's just for minutes, in the transition of the deed from buyer to seller. They receive and disperse all monies. All of the exchange mechanisms have strict time limits. In a 1031 exchange, you have forty-five days after closing to identify up to three potential like-kind replacement properties. They must be designated in writing via the facilitator. You have one hundred twenty days after the expiration of the forty-five day designation period to close on one or more of the replacement properties. In the meantime, the sales proceeds from the property sold are held by the facilitator. Cash not used for the purchase of the exchange property is returned to you as "boot". The cash never passes through your hands. Nor does the deed. The deed of the property sold goes from the facilitator and the facilitator gives you a deed to the new land.

Sound confusing? In reality it's not, but if you're not familiar with it, your first several exchanges can feel bewildering. Again, make sure you have a good team assembled that includes competent tax and legal counsel. They will know the good facilitators and exchange agents. The better your exchange agent, the smoother the transaction. And, the more secure your tax deferral.

From Twisty to Twisted

There's an even more complicated exchange animal in the deferred tax zoo. These are called Starker Exchanges. If you really want to have your eyes cross, dig into Reverse Starker Exchanges. That's when you buy going backward. Starker exchanges work well in situations where the replacement property cannot be purchased within the shorter time guidelines of the 1031. A good example: You are selling your land and residence, but instead of buying a new piece of land with an existing residence you want to build your dream house. Obviously your dream house can't be built in the approximate one hundred and sixty five day time allowed by a 1031. The Starker Exchange through various mechanisms, also involving a facilitator, extends that time frame out significantly. There is more paperwork, but it can buy you up to two years to use the funds on which you wish to defer taxes.

Reverse Starker exchanges are not used often, but there are situations in which they are the perfect solution for a seller who has a large real estate gain, wants it sheltered and has a specific real estate target in mind for acquisition, but the purchase can't be completed for one reason or the other for an extended period of time. There are exchange mechanisms which entail purchasing the exchange property *prior* to your sale of the property generating the gain you are deferring. There are several good websites on the reference page at the end of Volume One, if these concepts intrigue you and you wish to learn more about them. Again, I emphasize—no one should attempt a 1031 Exchange, a Starker Exchange, and particularly a Reverse Starker Exchange without professionals on your team who are familiar with those transactional processes.

The King of Them All—Conservation Easements

Section V of Volume One is dedicated entirely to conservation easements. There will be sections on conservation easements in all the volumes of *Land for Love and Money*, and the sections will be updated on the *Land for Love and Money* website and new editions of these volumes from year to year as conditions warrant.

Conservation easements can save you money on federal income tax and estate tax and, in certain states, on state income tax. In other states an easement can actually generate tax credits, the most valuable form of tax benefit.

- A deduction lessens your taxable income and therefore lowers your tax.
- A tax credit applies dollar for dollar against the tax bill you owe.

Credits generated by easements are highly transferable and salable in certain states. In Colorado, they can command up to 80 cents per dollar of credit. You may shake your head, but think about it. Somebody who's living in Colorado and has a high Colorado tax liability can buy the tax credit from the Grantor of a conservation easement who can't use it, pay 80 cents on the dollar in December and four months later, in April save 20 cents of tax for each dollar of credit they purchased. 5% a month or 20% over four months is not a bad return. Again, make sure you have people on your team who know the ins and outs. Treatment of conservation easements, deductions, and tax credits vary widely from state to state.

Since the 2003 Bush Tax Cuts, conservation easement grants have received extra favorable treatment. This will likely diminish, or may perhaps revert to the old pre-Bush levels of benefit in January

2013. That too is discussed in Section V.

It Doesn't Happen over Night

Conservation easements are not things that are in place at the snap of a finger. You must have held the property for a year and a day to get full market value for the donation. It takes time to locate the proper Grantee and negotiate the easement document. The negotiation of that document is critical not only to the success of the easement, but to the future value and salability of the property you're going to be encumbering with the easement.

Conservation Mineral Experts and Field Researchers or Hydrologists, Geologists, Biologists! Oh My!

There are a number of consultants who come out to check all aspects of the property, (kind of the due diligence of the Grantee.) In certain states, there will be mineral experts because mineral rights affect the drafting of the document and the grant. There will be field researchers who put together a baseline study indexing all of the resource attributes the property has as of a specific point in time. The baseline study is the document by which the Grantee monitors change on the property in perpetuity. In some ways it's also the control mechanism to make sure you don't do what the easement prohibits. If the property is collateral for loans, the banks or other lenders will have to subordinate to the easement for the easement to be effective. That also generally takes time to process or negotiate (unless you built the provision into your loan docs at closing). "PPPPP"!

If you put together a good team of competent professionals who are familiar with easements and you have a crackerjack, experienced Grantee (and no problems arise in the process), you can get an easement done from idea to recording in four to six months. If you're really lucky you may shave a month off that. The odds are it will take longer. Plan accordingly. An easement affects the entire year in which it is recorded. I'm chuckling. Like a divorce. I suppose you could say you are divorcing some of your property rights from your property. So an easement done on December 31 will shelter your income for the entire 364 days prior to that. There are other benefits too, in using conservation easements, which are discussed in other chapters.

Leaving a Preservation Footprint

Easements are unique in that you can leave a perpetual preservation footprint upon the land—which is highly gratifying, and you get paid to do the right thing. Not many opportunities in life carry that combination of existential, spiritual, and financial benefit. But if you don't do it correctly, you can strip all the value from your property and render it virtually unsalable. See Section V.

There is also what I call "money easements" available. This type of easement process is generally done through a government agency whose target is specific conservation values, such as along creeks and riparian areas. Some of these easement programs actually pay you for each year of the easement and additionally generate some tax benefit, but there are trade-offs to dealing with the government on an easement. You will have to weigh them for yourselves. Suffice it to say that in my forty years in real estate and many, many, conservation easements, we have never done one with the government.

There are yet other facets to tax savings. If you have mineral reserves, (oil, gas, etc.) there is "depletion." The purchase of certain equipment useful in land operations can generate tax credits. Alternative energy or energy savings installations for your rural home, irrigation system and other land related power needs can also earn you deductions, credits and grants.

Taxing the Wind?

Did you know of the tax on wind? It's coming! Wyoming actually passed a law, which is quite clever, in the last twenty-four months. The statute designates wind as a real estate asset that is appurtenant to the land. Wyoming real estate contracts now actually have boxes that need to be checked by the seller certifying to the buyer that the wind asset has not been severed from the property, i.e., leased to a wind power generator, for instance. Remarkable. However, can you think of any asset that is not taxed in some way? Nope. The tax on wind is coming.

One of These Days

Have I touched every aspect of real estate tax, or tax related to real estate tax land? No. But I hope I've afforded you a taste of some of the main tax components that can generate or save significant tax dollars in the purchase, sale and ownership phases of your land experience.

One of these days the tax code will be much simpler. It may hurt a bit at first, but it will streamline government, power up the economy, and increase revenues. It would not surprise me to see many of the tax mechanisms described above disappear. However for now, unfortunately for our country, but fortunately for the owners of land and real estate, the tax statutes continue headed for further convolution and continued new specialized niches of tax breaks designed to be enjoyed by the owners of land and structures.

SECTION IV

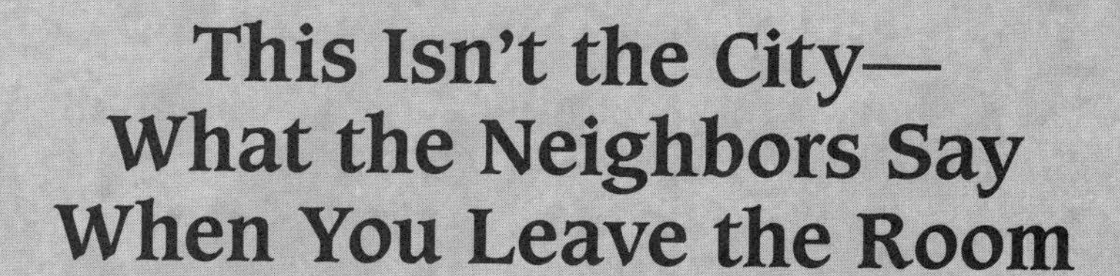

This Isn't the City—What the Neighbors Say When You Leave the Room

Chapter Sixteen
Small Towns: Americana for the Soul

Birds chirp, sunlight filters through shimmering leaves and deer delicately browse in grassy meadows. The Veteran's Day Parade consists of two fire trucks and three hay wagons pulled by pickup trucks converted to makeshift floats by the school kids. Rural lands and small towns are indeed idyllic. However, beneath the surface sometimes seethes a bubbling brew of politics, friendships, enmities, humor, rancor, rumor and occasionally envy—not unlike the dynamics of most families.

Like many aspects of life anywhere, life in rural areas is not black and white—the positives counterbalance the negatives. Yet I believe the attributes of small communities far outweigh the detriments. For those unfamiliar with small towns or the more sparsely settled areas outside the metropolitan cores, this section will be an amusing insight. The tips and experiences in this Section IV, and a sister section in Volume Two of *Land for Love and Money*, may save a landowner from a permanent *faux pas* within the community, assist you in quickly gaining respect and will certainly add to your overall enjoyment of your land and potentially wonderful small-town experience.

Some may argue this section is somehow "looking down" at small town personalities and life. Others may wrinkle their nose at the lack of "urban sophistication" of rural enclaves. Truth is, I love small towns, little bergs and rural enclaves, and most of the characters who inhabit them. There is no adequate way to describe a small town, Friday evening football game starring the local high school squad—no more than six to eight kids in the really tiny communities. The fading warmth and color of a setting sun, cool evening air caressing your skin, electric excitement of the crowd standing four or five deep around the perimeter of the gridiron, many folks still splattered with manure or smelling slightly of diesel.

There is a moment—the two teams lined up on either side of the field, the meager nightlights struggle with the dusk, when the "Star Spangled Banner" echoes in scratchy tones from an old, donated loudspeaker box sitting on a wobbly raised platform, when cowboy hats and farmers caps are held over the heart and there's not a whisper in the gathered throng, and our nation's flag snaps red, white and blue against a darkening sky and the first glimmers of night stars—that pride in our country and the nostalgia of Americana, is overwhelming. This sense of community, of being a small part of things greater than yourself, fills your spirit. At that moment, you thank God that you are standing in that spot, amongst friends, frozen in a magical minute in the inexorable passage of universal time.

Truth be known—I have tears in my eyes as I write these paragraphs. Small towns are great things.

Chapter Seventeen
With the Speed of Light

The first prerequisite for getting along in a rural community is to understand that everyone knows everyone else's business—or thinks they do. What vehicle you drive, when you pick up your mail, and the most recent mischief of your child are titillating tidbits for discussion. News, usually only partially correct, travels like the wind from a force-five hurricane. Truly, a whisper on the south side of Main Street is a scream on the north side of Main Street in one nanosecond. This lightning transmission of gossip, innuendo and scattered facts is not limited to just your community, but freely bounces around every little town in your area.

About twenty-five years ago, I was living in a small town in Colorado. My former wife, Darlene (who is still my very good friend), and I traveled north to Montana to see another friend of many years. We planned to do some fishing, riding, some scouting for the upcoming hunting season and relax and enjoy one of our favorite spots. Early in the trip, Bob drove Darlene and me into Sheridan, Montana, which was then a small town of about six hundred people. Bob pulled the truck up to the front of the IGA on Main Street in a long line of pickups, jeeps and horse trailers. Darlene was sitting between Bob and me. I had to run into the store to get a pack of gum and a coffee, a thirty-second in-and-out quick stop.

Bob's house, a delightful older frame cabin, was located on forty acres about five minutes from town. As we returned to the homestead and rolled up to his front door in a cloud of summer dust, he cut the engine. We could hear the phone ringing inside. While Darlene and I collected the gear, Bob jumped out and ran in to answer the call. He emerged ashen-faced a few minutes later.

At that time, Bob was dating a woman named Judy, who was going to graduate school in Missoula about two hundred miles north of Sheridan. In the brief thirty-second period while I disappeared into the IGA, Darlene and Bob sitting together shoulder-to-shoulder on the front seat was witnessed by Judy's cousin, who lived in Sheridan. She had called Judy's sister in Bozeman, eighty-seven miles to the northeast. The sister had in turn phoned Judy's mom in Billings, about three hundred miles to the east. The mother then rang Judy in Missoula, almost four hundred miles north and west of Billings. Bob related to us with wide eyes that it was Judy on the phone wanting to know, "Who the hell the babe was in the front seat with you?" News literally traveled a full circle of nine hundred miles in less than three hundred seconds. That's how small rural areas are.

The other side to this coin is that small communities have retained more of the frontier values that made America great. Rural folks are more likely to be self-reliant, instantly rally to help others in an emergency, and generally exhibit more common sense. This grass-root, neighbor-to-neighbor linkage and tight town bond, in my opinion, far outweighs the nosey, gossipy negatives.

Chapter Eighteen
Adam's Rib

The second equally important concept to grasp about sparsely settled areas is that everyone knows everyone, and most folks in some way , shape or form are related by blood or marriage to most of the rest of the population. Long before a new landowner arrives on the scene, most residents have formed an opinion about everyone else in town. The tentacles of interrelated prejudices, dealings, histories, friendships, adversaries and mutual back-scratching are intricate coils. Words uttered without consideration to the wrong person at the wrong time could unintentionally result in castigation by half of the population in the valley.

I have developed my own theory over the years about this social phenomenon of rural areas. I suppose one could find the same set of interactive rules and reality in tight-knit local neighborhoods in the big city, but I lack that experience.

I surmise that very early on in the developmental stage of a child who grows up in a small community, the kid invariably gets involved in some type of dispute with another youngster. Perhaps Tommy took Joey's truck in kindergarten class, or Sally grabbed Betty's doll during recess in first grade. The ensuing altercation teaches the children a life lesson. If Joey picks a fight with Tommy, he has then picked a fight with Tommy's friends, Tommy's siblings, Tommy's parents, their friends and family and so on. In towns of several hundred people or even several thousand, one event in a child's life teaches them that, in order to get along with the majority of people, it is usually best to withhold negative comments and shy away from topics of dispute.

While the romantic image of honest, level eyes that look into yours, and agreement on a deal sealed by a firm handshake, is true enough with many people in rural areas, it is also a mistake to place complete faith and confidence in such simplicity. The majority of small community inhabitants are absolutely terrific, upstanding, straightforward people. However, as in all locations, rural or urban, there is a percentage of the population who will tell you what you want to hear, but will not do what they say, or will say the opposite thing to someone else ten minutes later. They will not share with you what they really feel. They learned way back in kindergarten that this is the way to not be liked. Some folks feel regrettably compelled to spread misinformation about "the newcomer." Their perception is that such negativity is a step up the local social ladder at your expense.

My thoughts here are not intended as insults to rural communities. My heart is only happy in such enclaves. But reality cannot be ignored when making a sizable investment of energy, emotion, money and time in a rural property, especially if you plan to spend considerable periods, or the rest of your life there. My advice remains to keep your ears sensitively tuned, personal perceptions on full alert, eyes wide open and trust your gut. The true friendships you will make, and the sincere mutual respect you will share with some residents, form an important base for acceptance from the community at large.

I have gotten this right and I have also goofed. No matter how many properties I have owned or managed in small towns and rural communities, I can count on inserting my foot between my mandibles and munching on my toes from time to time.

Twenty-five years ago, I was still a resident of Colorado. Enthralled by the beauty of the Big Sky country, I spent as much time as possible fishing in Montana. I had made friends with several of the local ranchers who had places along the Ruby River and had received much-coveted permission to occasionally fish on their properties. One ranch family knew I was involved in real estate and had a farm and ranch background.

It was a warm summer evening, and while I was having a burger at the local joint, all six family members came over to talk with me. I will call them the "Jones." The Jones had encountered a problem. The mid-eighties were not kind years for agriculture. Ranchers and farmers around the United States had been exhorted by the federal government to grow and produce more, because "America was going to feed the world." The feds forgot to inform them of pending trade agreements with Canada and Mexico, which without warning, suddenly opened the U.S. markets to a competitive flood of foreign agricultural and bovine-based products. Interest rates were still high from the Carter recession; families who had taken on debt to expand based on the government's promises, found themselves strapped.

This family had run into a problem with financing for their mother cow herd at the local bank. They wanted to know if I had any advice, or if I could help. I have always been for the underdog, and not much partial to institutional monoliths, which are bureaucratic, often lack common sense, and are typically arrogant. I told them I would meet with their lender. My fee would be permission to hunt whitetail on their place that coming fall.

They collected their documents; I met with them and the bank officer. We put together a structure that they and the bank were both pleased with. This gave me great satisfaction.

A month or so later, during an evening ablaze with a crimson Montana sunset reflecting off the dimples of rising trout along a stretch of the Ruby, I was again asked for assistance. I didn't know the old rancher who owned the place very well, but I knew he was fourth-generation and worked the place with his sons. I was tying on a fly when I felt his presence. I turned and saw him about twenty feet behind me. I will refer to him as "Harry."

"You know your way around finance and ranch stuff?" Harry asked, without even a hello. Not exactly sure of where he was going with his question, I scrambled up the bank and sat down on a log. He sat beside me. I was shocked to see tears in his eyes.

"My dad, grandfather and great-grandfather were in land and cattle, and I have owned a couple of places myself," I said cautiously.

"I understand you helped the Jones with their cow deal." His twisted, calloused hands clasped together, clenching and unclenching. His elbows rested on his knees and his weathered face was dejectedly fixed on the ground between his boots. "My daughter is married to the Jones' oldest boy."

My eyes widened a bit with the revelation of connection. Harry poured out his story to me. We talked long into the dark of the evening. The Farm Credit Agency had taken his sprinklers, threatened to take his cows and had raised the specter of a lawsuit on the guarantee that he and all his sons had signed on the ranch. They were broke and he didn't know what to do.

From Harry's forlorn tale, I had the strong suspicion his lender had acted improperly. In synopsis, over the next nine months, for a fee of 3% of what I saved him, to be paid over time, I focused on helping this family. The lender had indeed imperiously and illegally breached its loan agreements. The sprinklers were returned, liens were released on the cows, a $2.2 million land debt was written down without litigation to a fraction of that amount, the personal guarantees were released and other matters beneficial to Harry and his sons were worked out.

I was flooded with calls thereafter by acquaintances and friends of Harry's. I am proud to say that in those years I helped over forty long-time ranch families stay on their ranches and revamp their operations to once again be viable in changing times. Besides enormous personal gratification, that group of people also formed the foundation of my friendships and what I call a small community goodwill nucleus.

There are times, however, when my intelligence falters. Harry's grandson played football for the local, tiny high school. Several years after I helped Harry with his financial workout, he invited me down to see his grandson play in a game against arch-rival Twin Bridges, just nine miles down valley. The sidelines were crowded. I found myself standing next to a gentleman with whom I exchanged a few friendly comments. The refs made a particularly bad call against Sheridan.

I said to the man next to me, "I wonder how much Twin is paying that ref! What a bad call!" There might have been an expletive in there, too.

His head snapped around and his eyes glared. "That's my brother!" he said and stomped away.

I found out the next day that not only was the referee his brother, but that his brother's brother-in-law owned the well-drilling company over in Butte that was going to drill a well on one of the ranches I managed. I was also informed in the following day's strained phone call from the brother-in-law that his two well rigs were suddenly really busy, and it would be years, if ever, before he would get one out to the ranch. I learned a quick lesson in watching what I say.

Fortunately, in the end, that turned out to be a good thing because I hooked up with the local driller in Sheridan, who has now drilled more than a score of wells for us over the ensuing years. He's terrific, very honest and has never yet punched a dry hole for any of our wells. As an aside, I found out the Sheridan well driller had gone to high school with the patriarch of the Jones clan. Small towns are small worlds indeed.

Chapter Nineteen
Fire Engines, Hospital Beds, and Goal Posts

You can gain respect in a small community by participating in local activities and organizations. This is also a great way to network and generate personal warm fuzzies. Little towns in sparsely settled areas are studies in dichotomy. Residents are typically fiercely independent. They are obviously averse to the throngs and cacophony of big cities and densely inhabited areas. Most non-resort area rural folks are suspicious of government and external controls and, with few exceptions, totally self-reliant.

The other side of that coin is that remote areas lack the infrastructure of suburbs, exurbs and metropolitan areas. Many services are funded almost entirely by a combination of community and local revenues from the town or county government. In many cases, important area functions would not exist without volunteer effort to assist the few paid professionals a small town, county or rural jurisdiction can afford to hire. Rural people are particularly pleased when newcomers show tangible interest via involvement or financial contribution, or both. Attention to the health clinic or small hospital, volunteer fire department and the local school system, particularly athletics, are surefire winners, generate personal good will and they're a pleasure to be involved with.

Rural volunteer fire departments are the backbone of public

safety. These organizations provide 911 assistance, paramedics and firefighting. Firefighting in outlying locales is not only about saving a house but also includes fighting grass fires and forest fires, and taking preventative measures in advance of controlled burns. Local volunteer outfits have saved my bacon on more than one occasion. Just in the last five years, twice in Montana and once in Wyoming, lighting strikes started fires closely adjacent to or on one of our ranches. The volunteer fire departments were out in minutes, even though the locations were in remote areas with extremely difficult access.

Back in Colorado three decades ago, my then business/ranch partner and I were completing our own house on our first ranch. We had constructed the dwelling lovingly, if not perfectly. We were part-time members of the local Rist Canyon Volunteer Fire Department. We drilled with the regulars, and once in a while participated in dousing several small fires.

We were putting the finishing touches on the home one hot August morning. The usual riveting view of the high country plains to the east of our timbered hill was obscured by heat haze. Dave, our nearest neighbor, lived a couple of miles and several canyons to the west. He came roaring down to the house and jumped from his beat up Toyota Land Cruiser with eyes wide. We quickly ascertained from his garbled shouts and wild gesticulations that there was a fire right over the ridge. Bob and I looked at each other, startled. Dave sped off in a cloud of swirling dust, sounding the alarm like Paul Revere of the mountain.

We grabbed shovels and our always-full seventy-pound Indian Tanks. These are contraptions that strap to your back and shoot rather diminutive sprays of water to arrest small brush fires. We ran to the pickup and careened up the rough four-wheel drive road to the ridge. We could see heavy dense smoke but could get the truck no further. We leapt out, hitched on the Indian Tanks, grabbed the shovels and a chain saw and hustled up the steep grade. We came over a rise in the topography and stopped, dumbfounded. The fire was roaring out of control, perhaps encompassing ten to fifteen acres. It was crowning, jumping from tree-top to tree-top. Each successive pine tree erupted in a gigantic explosive ball of heat and flame. Bob looked at me, pale and horror-stricken. I'm sure my expression was the same. Late summer meant tinder dry conditions and the pine needles on the forest floor formed a perfect fuel bed. We then glanced at our puny shovels and the diminutive nozzles hanging suspended from our belts running from the Indian Tanks on our backs. Without a word we turned and ran back down the ridge. We had not been trained for this.

The volunteer fire department arrived shortly thereafter followed by the forest service crew. After a week of aerial retardant and a grimy slug-it-out with persistent flames in a dangerous environment, we brought the fire under control. It had consumed about seven hundred fifty acres. We were filthy, soot-blackened and exhausted, as were our fellow firefighters, but not an acre of ours was burned, the house was safe and none of our neighbors lost anything of substance.

*****

Many towns or valleys are fortunate to have small health care units. There might simply be a clinic staffed by a rural doctor, perhaps several days per week. More fortunate towns have hospitals from ten to thirty beds, equipped to administer primary trauma care and keep someone alive for transport to a larger metropolitan area.

Still others belong to co-ops for several different communities with some medical and volunteer staffing.

These outposts of health care are a pleasure to deal with. I know. They have treated me for everything from a horse stepping on my toes to flu, kidney stones and, incredulous as it may sound, the proper diagnosis of a rare malady after five specialists in four hoity-toity city medical centers were unable to figure out the strange abnormality that had suddenly overcome me in the 1990s.

I had finally dragged myself to the doctor at the little clinic in Sheridan, wanting merely to refill the purely symptomatic non-curative medicines that the experts in the big city hospitals had prescribed. Doctor Madany, a young, very talented physician, listened intently to my explanation of symptoms. When I finished answering his questions, he rose from his desk, walked out of his office and two minutes later returned with a big, thick book. He ran his forefinger across the pages as he skimmed through sections. He stopped, read intently and looked up at me.

"You have Graves Disease," he said simply and with surety.

He was right. I had it treated a month later over at Bozeman Deaconess, a great regional hospital, and I have been fine ever since.

*****

And then there are the schools. Education is as much a hot topic in the outlying areas as it is in the suburbs or the inner city. The focus in small towns is different, though. One can be involved on both micro and macro levels. There are several avenues to achieve either. Little things like showing up for parent-teacher conferences are noticed. Remember, every teacher knows who you are, recognizes your vehicle and knows your kids. They are, after all, just one of the four to eight students in their class.

My children attended high school in such an academic environment. The entire school population, grades nine through twelve, was less than one hundred kids. My son's graduating class was twenty-three, and my daughter's seventeen. Teachers know if you don't show up for conferences. I am convinced that they keep a log of which parents call them to discuss poor grades, reasons for less than academic excellence and to request advice on how a parent can assist a child. This seemingly minor bit of community involvement says worlds about you to the school's staff, and they know everyone in town. More importantly, it is the right thing to do for your children.

There are other actions that demonstrate concern. If you have the courage, you can get elected to the local school board. Be forewarned that you will have both supporters and detractors, and a few who hate your guts. However, everybody will respect your involvement. Support local school functions. As one example, rural schools have FCCLA (Family, Career and Community Leaders of America) and FFA (Future Farmers of America). These great programs are half academic and half agrarian. Many chapters organize trips for their students to historical destinations, even Washington D.C., which my children were fortunate enough to experience. In addition to supporting your offspring with monetary donations to these school-based outfits, make sure you order generously from the local annual bake sales.

Then, of course, are the school sports. The fervor, excitement and the rabid support of local high school teams by the community rivals and perhaps surpasses anything one might see in professional or collegiate competition. The sons and daughters who comprise these six- or eight-player football, basketball, track and volleyball teams are the progeny of other local farmers, ranchers and rural property owners. The first and foremost rule for small-town athletics is attendance and interest. Friday night football games, Saturday volleyball tournaments and the twice-weekly track events of spring are all extremely well attended. The average event might well host two-thirds of the town. For the big events, such as football playoffs, conference championships or state championships, which my son was fortunate enough to enjoy, several thousand people show up for games from all across the state. And, if you have a fairly good team, it is absolutely the talk of the town. As I remember the struggling teams that got their share of discussion, too.

I mostly kept a low profile with my kids' mentors and coaches. Every once in a while, I would make a suggestion, but that was the exception rather than the rule. Small town athletics are very much turf-driven. However, it is of immense benefit to your team, your children, your friends children, the community and yourself, to contribute your time and money generously. There is usually a local athletic boosters club for the high school teams. Join, donate and enjoy the experience. Attend awards banquets. These are big things for the kids, and even more important to the parents. So much the better if your son or daughter is the recipient of an award or two. With the entire varsity and junior varsity squads combined typically consisting of ten to fifteen kids, chances are everyone will get a trophy!

If your child does not participate in athletics, it is likely they will be involved in academic or creative groups. My daughter was editor of the school paper, won competitions in state-wide art contests and with others, put together the senior yearbook. I advertised in the school newspaper and yearbook, contributed to various fundraisers and enjoyed the camaraderie of the other parents at school plays and ceremonies.

Contribute behind the scenes. I would always call the coaches early in the year and inquire if there was anything in particular that the team needed. Alternatively, I would ask my kids to ask the coaches and teachers. I allowed the use of some of my photography in presentations and publications. I bought a lot of uniforms and helmets for the football team.

In my son's senior year, the state championship track meet was held in Helena during two days of torrential rain. Fine athletes from all over the state would have done better wearing swimming suits and goggles rather than track shoes. It was miserable. One of the other parents and I went to the local Walmart, purchased several dozen towels (in the team colors of purple and white), umbrellas, rain parkas and ponchos for the team and the parents. To this day I still get smiles and thanks for that. Sometimes the opportunity arises to contribute simple but special efforts that stand out in everyone's minds for years.

*****

My son and I were perched on the ridge with our binoculars, glassing for big bucks one cloudy afternoon late in hunting season. We watched with amazement from our hilltop perch as two men furtively crossed the river onto our place from the neighbors, stuffed their orange vests into camouflage knapsacks strapped to meat packs and set off to obviously sneak around in forbidden places.

With stealth, Rhett and I tailed them. When we finally walked up to them, took their rifle and bid them to follow us back to our truck, it was apparent that they had killed something somewhere on our ranch. They were extremely nervous about their situation. Perhaps they had no licenses, or perhaps they had shot an illegal animal. I decided not to inquire. Whatever was dead was dead, and the game warden would figure it out.

As we walked toward the truck one of them turned to me with an apprehensive twitch and said, "What would it take for you to forget that you ever saw us here?" The other added with a tremulous voice, "You don't need to call the sheriff, we can make this right."

Rhett and I glanced at each other. I decided to play stupid. "Well, you are clearly breaking the law. You are not just trespassing. You are a mile inside our boundary. By the looks of those meat packs, and only one of you carrying a rifle, I would say that you have killed something too." The oblique probe made the muscles in their faces tense.

"We'll pay you a trophy fee," stammered one of the men.

"Not interested, and a trophy fee does not breathe life into whatever carcass is lying up there on the hill, does it?" I shot back.

"Would five thousand dollars make it go away?" one of the men blurted out.

With effort, I tried to appear nonchalant. When we reached the truck, I turned to them. "I'll tell you what. Lots of ranches around here charge trespass fees for hunting. I'm going to waive that fee, if, you make a generous donation to the Sheridan School District Panther Football Team and personally deliver it to the coach tomorrow morning by nine a.m. If we ever see you inside our fence line again, we will throw the book at you, including whatever you did here."

The men agreed. We took their names and phone numbers from their licenses. They stumbled back up the hill.

The next morning the football coach called me. "I had these two really jumpy guys come to the school today. They dropped off a check for two thousand dollars to the football team. Would you happen to know anything about that?"

I indulged in a hearty laugh and replied, "Nope, wouldn't know anything about it, but I'm sure the money will be put to good use."

The coach chuckled and hung up. That story quickly became legend around town, was the subject of great amusement on the football team and endeared me to the parents of the team, with whom I enjoyed friendships on long road trips to distant tiny hamlets, sharing the thrills of our children's competition.

Chapter Twenty
The Uproar

Rest assured that at some point, ownership of rural property will result in involvement in an issue that will ignite, and unite, the community. It may be an intrusion of state or federal regulations. It may be a change in zoning or land use. Some misguided government jurisdiction may try to take, alter or influence water rights. The hubbub will most certainly affect the area's property rights, property values or both.

It is critical is these situations to become involved, first, to protect yourself, and second, to support your neighbors against a common threat. I generally refer to large bureaucracies having little comprehension, no compassion and distant myopic mindsets as "monoliths." I am not partial to monoliths. You will find that the huge majority of people in rural areas do not think kindly of them either. Nor are they sanguine when their rights are trampled, their voices not heard or their lands or property rights disturbed, altered, or taken.

These takings and other governmental intrusions, whether outright or indirect, are an accelerating trend due to current national politics and policies, and the populist mentality of certain states. Canada, on the other hand, appears to be moving towards increased protection of private property, particularly in British Columbia and Alberta. In the current environment, increased diligence is mandatory. Keep your ears carefully tuned to the hum in the tracks.

These situations, when they invariably arise, can be invaluable opportunities to become part of the community, help yourself and help others. Standing shoulder-to-shoulder with neighbors who share common goals and common foes will cement friendships with respect. Our ancestors banded together to vanquish mastodons. The key to killing modern monoliths is also unity. It is the bundle of sticks theory. An individual stick is easily snapped. A bundle is impossible to break.

Within the alliance that assembles against a monolithic foe, there will be certain people who can lend special skills to the collective effort. Experience, contacts, knowledge and the ability to organize or be an energetic participant in the initial organization are all important. Delegation of these key skills, and formulation of the kill-the-monolith strategy as soon as possible after the threat is known, are critical to success. Be proactive. If you know how to help the collective, volunteer. Do what you say. Accomplish any missions you accept. This type of involvement can even sway some of those who previously did not like or respect you.

As an example, utility companies are monoliths. If backed by federal government largesse—usually without oversight by more localized government hungry for revenue—utilities are extremely dangerous. Quite recently the federal government beat drums and sounded trumpets heralding a concerted push toward alternative and renewable energy forms. This unorganized, unplanned, largely subsidized[1] very political frenzy affects or will affect the majority of rural lands in the

[1]Google-a) Alternative Energy Subsidy-Federal Stimulus; b) Wind Power Federal Subsidy; and c) Government Subsidy to Alternative Energy Generation and Transmission.

U.S. The clouds of this perfect monolithic storm will cast shadows over tens of thousands of landowners in the coming years.

I could wax eloquent here about the fact that the federal government admits that under the best circumstances, less than 20% of our energy demand by 2030 will be able to be provided by wind and solar. I could also write pages on the fallacy of dumping huge sums of money as repayment to campaign contributors in the form of grandiose subsidies to make non-profitable alternative energy "viable" in the marketplace. Wind and solar, for example, requires one hundred and one times and sixty-four times (respectively), the subsidy to fossil fuels to be affordable. In actuality, I like renewable resources, but they need to be carefully planned, constructed in the proper locations and pursued in ways that do not undermine other industries and economics. One cannot save the environment by ruining the land.

The key to renewables is the transmission of the power generated to a market that can use it. Generally, areas most conducive to solar and wind are remote. Forty-story-high wind turbine towers and square miles of solar collectors are more often than not located on large expanses of lands far from transmission lines. The utilities claim crisscrossing the entire country with gigantic twelve-to-eighteen-story, monstrous steel power line towers is an absolute necessity. This hodgepodge, largely uncoordinated assault is driven by time limits that mandate commencement of construction, at the threat of losing federal cash, grants and tax incentive programs. Many projects are poorly planned, and the NEPA (National Environmental Policy Act) guidelines often massaged or ignored. These subsidies have led many transmission companies to focus on the creation of *future* opportunity zones for wind or solar developers, rather than satisfaction of current demand. General Electric, as the largest manufacturer of wind turbines and solar panels, is not shy about asserting its considerable political weight in Washington. Some of the prettiest wilderness areas in the country are at risk of industrialization.

One of these projects was the so-called Gateway Project, a multi-power line routing by three monolithic utilities across Idaho, Wyoming, Utah and Colorado. (For more information on this, see www.gatewaywestproject.com.) Two of the proposed lines were looped transmission corridors running from, and then back to, the major corridor. The loop was to run eighty miles through some of the most pristine country in the West and the most untrammeled and unspoiled lands within three hours of the Denver metro area. The routes aggressively proposed through this rugged wilderness consisted of eighteen-story steel towers every thirteen hundred feet with a road to every tower. The intent was simply to provide opportunity for potential future construction of four hundred-foot tall, two hundred eighty-foot wide wind turbines down this mountain corridor.

Arguments by the power companies that this construction was important to save us all from environmental degradation withered in the face of suddenly united opposition, which rallied to protest the negative physical and visual impact and the material adverse consequences to wildlife, watersheds, agriculture and recreation, as well as the negative impact on cultural and historic areas of significance. Two hundred or so ranch owners organized pretty quickly into the Northern Laramie Range Alliance (NLRA)[2], which continues to grow.

[2]www.nlralliance.org

Hopefully, your due diligence, investigation and common sense will ensure you never face a sinister macro threat to the land you love and its value. However, the unknown can always occur. If it does, the NRLA is a case study in how to proceed for success, as well as mistakes to avoid.

Certain members of the alliance were well-connected and had previously been legislators in Wyoming. Others had contacts on the national level. To those members of the group fell the responsibility of legislative government interaction. One of our firm's specialties is conservation, including cultural and historic matters. We took on the mission of organizing a number of ranchers at a very narrow neck of the valley, through which the transmission line would have to pass. We organized consultants and assisted neighbors in preparation of detailed maps, which included numerous points of historical, cultural and Native American designation.

Finally, the goal of public galvanization flowed to other well-connected ranchers in the area. They did an extremely effective job of rallying public support from Douglas, Cheyenne and Laramie.

A few of us with experience in business litigation were entrusted to bring a legal action that challenged the very foundation of the monolith's proposal. At the outset, this attack took the form of a request to the court to declare that the power companies did not have the right of eminent domain. In the course of the back-and-forth discussions with the utility companies, federal agencies, state agencies and landowners, I met many people. Some had heard of our ranches and some had not. Our base of friends, acquaintances, allies and network of mutual respect greatly expanded.

Demonstrating that organized opposition can prevail, the proposal for the unnecessary loop was abandoned by the power companies in mid-2009, in the face of stiff organized resistance. One other line was defeated, as were several turbine farms.

However, the NRLA also lost several key battles. The reasons for less-than-total victory were four. Be alert to these and avoid them in your group:

- Some of the wealthier, more powerful members of the group focused on steps most likely to protect their own lands. This created resentment in other group members.
- Many landowners were informed of discussions or negotiations affecting their lands after the fact. They were not pleased.
- In typical small town fashion, some owners did not want to anger a minority of ranchers who did want wind power, and did not want to "stand out" as being overly negative. There is no way to win a monumental battle such as this by being in the least bit timid.
- Most members of the group were reluctant to use the courts as one of the weapons in their arsenal.
- Last, but very importantly, the group did not hire an administrative person. The result was lack of communication, untimely communication and many missed opportunities on the local political level, which would have beneficially affected eminent domain, alternative energy zoning, mapping and guidelines, moratoriums and overall public knowledge and support. Remember this old adage: "A single stick can be broken, but a bundle of sticks cannot."

If you are still searching for that special piece of land, open your eyes to what is happening politically in the regions of your search. If you have already purchased your piece of heaven, get involved and stay involved.

The satisfaction of being part of a successful strong communal effort on the right side of an issue is incalculable. Friendships and alliances created will benefit all involved for years or decades to come. The respect gained from having the courage to voice suggestion and opinion, to play an active role in the plan and to fight for the resource, cannot be measured. The preservation of your own property rights and values are worth protecting. Avoidance of emotional trauma inherent to being witness to land you love being ripped apart by mindless greed and lackadaisical planning of disinterested third parties is incalculable.

In summary, when an occasion like this arises, and odds are it will in the course of your stewardship of your property, get involved. Lend your shoulder to the common wheel.

Chapter Twenty-One
Cows Gone Wild

I never cease to be amazed at what some folks will do to get their cattle on someone else's grass. Sometimes, more insidiously, livestock can be used as a weapon of advantage or persuasion. If you have rural property in an area where there is livestock, chances are that at some time your livestock is going to be on somebody else's place or vice versa. This is particularly true of horses and yearling steers. Those critters like to roam and "push fence." Mother cows with calves like easy feed and are unlikely to move unless they are out of grass or, are moved.

*****

It was a tranquil Indian summer day. Sunlight filtered through pine needles and the golden red of quaking aspen leaves. I had been on a horse since four a.m. and hiked an additional three miles through a morning frost, resulting in an energy-sucking chill. No great bull elk had shown himself in this remote inviting canyon bisected by a small creek. I planned to camp there the whole day and steal out after dark. I enjoyed a mid-day siesta in the drowsy warmth.

I was awakened by a wet rasp-like caress on my cheek, along with a less than thrilling smell I quickly realized was bad breath. The kiss of an inquisitive cow jerked me awake. Apparently my nodding head must have resembled a salt block. I don't know who jumped the highest, me or the cow. I recovered from my surprise and was truly annoyed. I was more than two miles from the nearest property line of our Wyoming ranch, inside an area that we had gone to great pains and expense to fence in order to protect the restored riparian habitat. Yet here was a neighbor's cow along with about twenty of her cousins in exactly the wrong place at exactly the wrong time.

I checked the brands. They belonged to the family who leased National Forest lands on the eastern boundary of our spread. I had had numerous run-ins with that federal lessee over the previous five years. The man simply did not want to live up to his responsibility to fix the fence between us and the forest land, although that was part of his federal lease agreement. Over the years, we had wasted many days rounding up his cows and trying to talk some sense into him. Our complaints to the Forest Service sometimes resulted in temporary action, but never had any long-term result.

We had resorted to driving the cows all the way through the ranch to the county road where they could wander for miles, which made his roundup more difficult. We had intimated that the "next time" it happened, his cows might become permanently lost or mysteriously disappear somewhere in the interior of our acreage. Our neighbor sometimes pandered to our concerns. Once in a while he would send his sons up to fix a few hundred yards of the five-mile excuse for a fence. But generally he just ignored us. After all, grass is money and the other guy's grass is free.

For a brief instant that day in the canyon I contemplated beef rather than elk steaks that night. I was annoyed enough by that cow's foul-smelling tongue and the numerous trespasses of half a decade that I marched out of the canyon back to the horse, rode down to the cabins that we use as spike camp in that high country, jumped in the truck, and roared the twenty miles to the lower ranch house where we had some communication capabilities.

The phone finally in hand, I called the patriarch of the family who had the forest lease. Even though Wyoming is a "fence out" state* I could feel the animosity when I told him who was on the other end of the line.

"How many times have we asked you to keep your cows off our place?" I demanded.

"Well, we have talked about it a bit and you know I sent the boys up there to fix the fence," he drawled.

"BS. Your boys have not fixed five hundred yards of fence out of five miles in over five years. Last year we spent the equivalent of six man-days chasing your cows back onto your lease or down to the county road. This is our time, our money and our grass. The Forest Service has been on you, we have been on you, and other neighbors have been on you. The bottom line is you don't control your cows and you don't care because there is really no ramification."

"Well, we are really busy on the home place and that is about forty miles away, as you know…" he stammered.

"Well, I am done," I interrupted him. "I don't know if you know what that means, 'Sam', since you don't know me well, but it means exactly what it sounds like. I am done! Here is what you are going to do. You are going to go up and get every single cow, and it looks like there is about twenty pair, off of our property by noon tomorrow. You are going to bring your sons. And they are going to start fixing that entire five miles of fence tomorrow, and they are not going to stop until they are done.

* An owner is responsible for fence to keep livestock out, rather than vice versa. U.S. Forest Service leases, however, require the lessee to maintain all fencing in and around the leased federal ground.

If you miss any of those deadlines, here is what we are going to do. First, we are going to file an Agisters Lien on your brand. Every time you sell one of those heifers, or any of those steers, you are going to pay us on the lien. The lien is going to be for all of your trespasses for the past five years, including today. We have kept a log and I bet you it is between three and four thousand animal unit days, which is about one hundred fifty AUMs. Our rate is going to be $100 per AUM, which is about what it costs when you get done with our time, aggravation, expense and damage." I could feel the head of steam as it boiled up from deep within my chest.

"But—" he tried to interject.

"I am not done." I knew my voice decibels were rising. "In addition, the next time one of your cows is on our place, unless it got through a portion of the fence because a tree fell over, we are going to call our attorneys and we are going to sue you for civil trespass and the damages associated with that. I will let you think about it. My math says the cost of your two boys fixing five miles of fence versus the cost of attorneys, five years of trespass and other problems and damages which are sure to arise is a deal. I bet you come to the same conclusion as me. It is way cheaper to be a good neighbor, fix the fence and maintain it." I hung up.

The fence did indeed get fixed within the required time frames. That was three years ago, and except for a few occasions which were simply unavoidable or for which "Sam" cannot be faulted, his cows have not tasted our grass since that conversation.

I can also relate tales of very different reactions to livestock trespass by truly concerned and well-meaning neighbors. I had a neighbor in Colorado some years back whose yearlings got into some of our high country. I had to talk him out of going up there in the dark at great risk to his sons, himself and their horses. I told him that the next day would be just fine. His wife baked three absolutely yummy apple pies for us as payment for their one-day indiscretion.

*****

We had a neighbor next to another of the Colorado ranches. He was building a fine new home on one hundred acres that tied into one corner of our larger place. I got a call one night in 2009 from his hysterical wife. Our pasture lessee's cows had somehow gotten on his property and were thoroughly enjoying the new construction underway.

The house was framed at that time. The cows had taken a particular fancy to the living room area and were happily camped out on the plywood floors. It seems they liked the view to the west towards the Grand Mesa. Those windows were covered with slobber marks from their noses as they pressed their faces against the glass, no doubt trying to take in the sunset. After the fact, it was my theory that the open floor plan had attracted them to that level of the house. Who says cows don't have taste?

The next morning, we all met out there. Apparently one of the contractors had taken out a portion of the fence and brace posts to get in a large piece of equipment. This created an open gap between his property and ours. We had given his contractor permission to cross us since it was a shorter run for him during the construction period. We extricated the cows from the abode. The roundup was on foot to minimize any more damage to the floors. Our neighbor apologized for the drama, sheepishly admitted that it had been his mistake not to notice the hole in the fence created by his own contractors, and together we made the repair. Mission accomplished and everyone was smiles. I assume they power-sprayed their subfloors before putting down the carpet!

*****

Many western states have "fence-out laws." In other words, if you do not construct a fence to keep the neighbor's livestock off your grass, too bad for you. Open Range Laws in some of the western states and in western Canada also contribute to trespass as cows move up and down county or provincial right of ways from one property to another. The eastern states and provinces generally take a different view. If you have animals, you are responsible for them and for the enclosures that keep them on your property and not someone else's.

Whatever the state or provincial law, the reality is that livestock will from time to time escape. Trees will fall on fences. Big game animals will knock strands of wire off posts or in some cases flatten the fence entirely. Animals that have depleted forage on one side of a fence will obviously want to get to the other side of the fence to partake in more ample feed supplies. High water or beaver activity can wipe out a boundary along water courses.

If it is your animals trespassing, do the right thing and do it promptly. Call your neighbor and inform them of the indiscretion. Move them back onto your place immediately. Repair the breach from which they escaped. Offer compensation to your neighbor whether in the form of cash, helping them out on their place, or a scrumptious neighborly apple pie. This will earn you respect and good will in the community. Remember, word travels quickly. In return, your neighbors will be as rapid in their response as you are in yours.

If your property becomes the victim of an unwitting trespass, let the owner of the livestock know immediately. Be friendly though firm, and follow up to make sure that they perform the agreed-upon rectification within the time frames discussed. Perhaps you could use the opportunity to suggest and agree on a plan to avoid the situation in the future. This might be as simple as the two of you meeting once or twice a year, walking or riding the fence together and then sharing the expense of the repairs. Each of you can agree to alternating years in fix-up responsibilities. Many times neighbors meet in the middle of a fence line, and each person agrees to fix the fence to his or her left or right.

If you find yourself in the unfortunate situation where a neighbor or adjoining landowner tries to take advantage of the situation, or their attitude is one of obvious unconcern, do not hesitate about getting firm, immediately. Be reasonable, but state the expected resolution explicitly, and how to avoid similar dilemmas in the future. Follow up with a letter in writing. If the situation reoccurs, get tough. The Agisters Lien on a rancher's brand and civil remedies for trespass and damages almost always does the trick. Less than honorable folks have been known to get religion overnight when they face an expense greater than grazing their animals on their own grass.

Bear in mind, whether you have a spread of many thousands of acres, or a five- to twenty-acre place in some of the more crowded areas of the continent, the protection of your resource, your grass and your water is important to your sanity, to your values and indeed to the health of your own livestock. An owner who has twenty acres back east with four or five horses and who plans to support those horses year-round on that place with pasture and supplemental winter hay will be in a serious pickle indeed if the neighbor's stock get in the fence for a day or two. It doesn't take long for just a few trespass animals to blaze ten acres of grass down to the nubs.

SECTION V

Conservation—Getting Paid to Do the Right Thing

Chapter Twenty-Two
What Is a Conservation Easement?

It is not often that one gets to leave the imprint of perpetual preservation on a significant chunk of the planet in the form of conservation of rapidly disappearing prime resources. As well as enjoying the attendant financial consideration in the form of tax benefits that emanates from a grant, there is the additional satisfaction of getting paid to do the right thing.

But there is a dark side to the grants of these conservation easements. Their use by unscrupulous or ignorant grantors can be shady. Grants by unsophisticated landowners being advised by sometimes well-meaning but usually ill-informed advisors or consultants can be disastrous. Few attorneys and CPAs know much about this process, and they often fail to comprehend that a good long-term plan, with flexible strategies and quantifiable goals, is integral to the formulation of a successful grant or series of easements on any piece of property. Potential benefits and adverse effects apply to property anywhere and of any size. To be meaningful and legal, and to serve the purpose of resource protection, a conservation easement must achieve Real Conservation Value.

It's important that anyone considering a grant understands what a conservation easement really is. The granting of conservation easements is governed by Section 170 of the Internal Revenue Code

(IRC-170). This voluminous statute has been updated and improved, mostly to the benefit of the Grantors (persons donating an easement), by code clarifications over the years and through congressional acts. It is obviously a detailed and complicated piece of law, full of nuances, which will be explained only on a general business basis here. I cannot emphasize strongly enough how important it is to have qualified, experienced advisors, including an attorney and CPA who are familiar with easements, who fully understand these great tools and who can think big-picture and long-term. The advisors and/or the grantor must comprehend the potential material adverse and perpetual effects grants can have on land, land values and exit strategy if used improperly or without proper prior planning.

Few people understand conservation easements. Easements are highly negotiable prior to grant. If carefully formulated, they can simultaneously be very valuable tools in tax savings, accomplish important resource goals, beneficially affect preservation and can increase certain long-term real estate values if properly phased and located. There is a common belief that a grant affords public access, or strips all the rights from a property. These myths could not be further from the truth. Conservation easements are a widely used, greatly expanding form of preservation with financial incentive. They are highly negotiable. If done correctly, they are value-adding instruments over time, and contribute to environmental safeguards, which beneficially affect not only the property on which the easement is placed, but the entirety of the local ecosystem.

In simplest terms, a conservation easement is the grant (donation) by the Grantor (landowner) of certain rights of ecological value to a Qualified Grantee (the organization that accepts the donation). Every property has a bundle of rights. You can build roads on it, subdivide it, sell or transfer it in pieces, mine it, strip it, timber it, farm it, improve it, etc. Just as a donation of an art piece to an art museum carries certain tax benefits, so, too, do property rights have donative value. The appraised value of the bundle of potential rights donated becomes a tax deduction, which can be extremely beneficial to the Grantor. Many Fortune 500–1000 companies, such as Plum Creek, International Paper and Wal-Mart, have become heavily involved in conservation easement grants. Many states give tax credits, in addition to the Federal deductions. Credits directly lower tax owed. If you owe $20,000 in tax, and have a $10,000 credit, your tax liability drops to $10,000. Deductions lessen taxable income. If you have $200,000 in Adjusted Gross Income (AGI) on the bottom line of your tax schedule and you have a $50,000 deduction to apply, your AGI is then $150,000, and your tax liability is computed on the lower amount.

Easements differ from standard real-estate-related write-offs in that the deductions or credits flow to and stay with the Grantor, not the property. One could literally grant an easement on Monday, sell the property on Tuesday and still maintain the tax benefits of the grant.

Many federal agencies, states, counties and now local municipalities are involved in the grant of easements. Many jurisdictions require easements on subdivided property to maintain open space, agriculture, wildlife, fishery and habitat values. When a conservation easement is negotiated, certain of the bundles of rights can be donated, and certain of the bundles of rights can be reserved. These are "Reserved Rights." Done properly, reserved rights can generate very significant flexibility related to future tax, real estate and conservation value for an owner or subsequent purchaser.

Contrary to popular misconceptions, what conservation easements DO NOT DO, unless the landowner specifically agrees otherwise, are the following:

- Easements do not restrict hunting, fishing or recreation.
- They do not afford the public any access whatsoever.
- Even the Grantee cannot come on the property without the permission of the owner except in extraordinary circumstances.
- Properly done, easements do not restrict rights which are properly reserved, including all recreation rights, rights to subdivide ("transfer") or sell (or donate in the future for additional tax deduction) already existing parcels, build additional homes and structures, continue to farm, extract minerals or timber, build ponds and conduct other resource/ agricultural wildlife improvements, guest ranch, etc.
- A conservation easement completed through a private Grantee does not afford any government entity at any level any increased jurisdiction, rights, entry or management oversight on the property. The government is not involved in such cases.

Chapter Twenty-Three
The Soul and Dollars of Preservation: The Easement Epiphany

In the go-go days of the early eighties, I had already been heavily involved in resource-oriented urban and exurban development for ten years. A hectic time, I needed twenty-eight hours in every twenty-four-hour day. I never lost sight of my roots though, and my first love remained the small ranches I owned. Even though I was chairman of the billion-dollar development company I had founded at the age of twenty-one, I generally wore a flannel shirt and cowboy hat, and drove a pickup, much to the consternation of my board of directors. Certain times of the year, I would slap the camper on the back of the truck, perhaps hitch up the horse trailer or drift boat and disappear for weeks. I was relegated, though, to hunting and fishing mostly public lands, because my ranches were too small and too close to the anthill of humanity known as the Front Range of Colorado. I hungered for a big place that was my own that I could improve, preserve, enjoy, run some cows on and get lost in.

I was approached by a well-meaning and hard-working rancher, Carl Judson, who was looking for investors in a sixteen-thousand-acre spread known as Phantom Canyon Ranch, located half an hour's drive north of Fort Collins. It was an incredible property, with varying ecosystems, low mountain foothills punctuated with spires of rock and red granite cliffs pock-marked by the vibrant green of rock lichen. Stands of pines and north slope aspens spread in clusters up the rolling toes of the Rockies. Through it all ran a magical, invisible, deeply-formed canyon. Miles of the North Fork of the Cache La Poudre River coursed through the bowels of the chasm. The North Fork was reputed to be, by those fortunate few who had fished there, a blue-ribbon wild fishery. I toured the ranch, hiked into the secret recesses of the canyon and was delighted by the seclusion. I became one of the largest partners.

A few years later I got a call from Carl. He wanted to know what I thought about donating a conservation easement to the Nature Conservancy on a portion of the ranch in order to protect the secret canyon. Carl suggested that subsequent sales of a few building sites outside the confines of the easement might generate money for the partnership, and could expand the scenarios under which the ranch might ultimately be sold in parcels to its partners.

Carl had researched conservation easements and had had discussions with the Nature Conservancy. In retrospect, he meant well, but it was a novel concept, and none of us could fully understand the consequences of the plan he was setting in motion. Little did I know that his phone call would forever change my perceptions of land use, preservation and land economics. Nor did I realize right then how that watershed moment would stimulate my intrigue with the concept, engender my resulting research and intertwine with a previous epiphany back in 1972 when I was nineteen.

* * * * *

On that June evening in 1972, my buddy Bob was behind the wheel of an F-250, intent on reaching the Madison River in time to fish. I was in the co-pilot's seat. In front of me, the open glove compartment door formed a tray for the fly-tying equipment, where I was industriously turning out big brown stonefly nymphs. Bob and I were making our annual Colorado-to-Montana pilgrimage to fish Bear Trap Canyon of the Madison River, prior to the salmon fly hatch. Around us, the verdant green of coming summer valleys swept into snow-capped peaks, and the grey-blue of sage covered the flanks of the late spring mountainsides.

The F-250 was screaming through the Ruby Valley on US-287. I gazed out the window and admired the grandeur of the place. It was near dusk and the fading sun had painted shadows, which sharply etched the contours and canyons, draws and washes and the flow of the topography. One huge chunk of land on the flank of the Tobacco Roots called to me, even from miles away. Stunned, I pointed out the window and said matter-of-factly, "One day I'm gonna own that ranch."

Bob looked at me with one eyebrow raised and a bemused half smile. With a somewhat deprecating tone, he responded, "We need ten more stone flies and we're only a half an hour from the river. Stop talking. Get tying."

Twenty-six years after it spoke to me that dusky spring evening in the F-250 headed to the Madison River, several partners and I purchased that large, remarkably beautiful swath of the west face of the Tobacco Roots, with plans to restore the vitality of that sadly degraded working ranch, enhance its resources and preserve the same through conservation easement grants.

* * * * *

In 1991, one of the ranch outfits with which I was involved listened to my first presentation of the idea of a conservation easement and the win-win benefits for both the land and the landowners. They were swayed by my enthusiasm and gave me the green light to go ahead with the grant. It was my first experience with the proactive design and negotiation of a Conservation Easement Grant.

I have been involved as a consultant with no ownership stake, or as principal (owner) in scores upon scores of completed, or intended easements involving a number of national and local conservation trusts in two foreign countries and a host of western states including Colorado, Wyoming and Montana. These easements have conserved or will conserve tens of thousands of acres of critical fisheries and wildlife habitat, ranch lands and agricultural properties in perpetuity.

Chapter Twenty-Four
Reserved Rights: Key to Future Flexibility and Value

Easement donative value can often be maximized if easements are granted on a phased basis. This requires good long-term planning. If granted with carefully thought-out reserved rights in the first round, a conservation easement can leave very significant increments of real estate and tax value realizable through easements on the rest of the property, or second-tier easements, or amendments to the initial easement. These can be enjoyed by a new owner, or the original Grantor.

Whether one is the Grantor of the conservation easement on a twenty- to one-hundred-acre piece of land somewhere back east, where zoning or other government overlayment might allow typical lot or small acreage subdivision (three and one-half houses per acre—aka 3.5/DU), or the Grantor of total or partial easements on a large ranch of many thousands of acres in the western part of the continent, the basic principles related to intelligent, effective granting and reservation of rights remain inviolate.

Reserved rights can afford a purchaser excellent land use and operational latitude. Inclusion of the following reserved rights and protections should be ensconced in some form in the grant of every easement. An actual Grant of Conservation Easement deed negotiated with a major National Land Trust is included in the *Green for Green* workbook. Reserved rights should include, as a minimum:

1) The right to construct and operate all beneficial agricultural improvements and structures, and implement all beneficial agricultural improvements including pasture, farming, fencing, irrigation and other improvements.

2) The right to operate and enjoy any and all property-related recreational and agricultural activities including guest ranching, lodging or eco-tourism activities, as well as farming or ranching activities such as livestock, crops and pasture.

3) The right to construct and maintain any and all beneficial resource improvements, such as restoration, creation or rehabilitation of ponds, springs, streams and fisheries; upland improvements for birds, wildlife, and livestock; and to conduct and profit from any and all private or reasonable commercial recreation, hunting and fishing rights permitted by the state law.

4) The right to build all roads necessary to reach residences, including driveways; and to construct and maintain improvements, such as drilling wells, installing septic tanks (pursuant to county regulations) and making similar resource-conscious limited-residential development-type improvements.

5) The right to retain small-acreage building envelopes legally described and excluded from the easement, and/or floating building sites, located anywhere on the ranch.

6) The right to construct a home, additional guest cottage or cabin, and non-residential outbuildings, such as a residence garage, shed, barn, etc. in each building envelope.

7) The right to exclude any and all public access, as the owner wishes.

Inherent in reserved rights is the right to donate, in a second-tier or easement amendment or series of amendments, either all or a portion of these many reserved rights. These future donations can be extremely valuable. Remember, however, that reservation of rights within any grant will reduce the donative (tax) value of the specific donation in which the rights were reserved.

This type of phasing strategy can result in a very significant escalation of tax benefits. As resource, agricultural and other improvements are completed on the property, values of future donations are likely to rise. The grant of easements can also increase the value of adjacent lands not subject to easement, and of the rights that have been reserved. Depending upon the individual Grantor's tax status, this strategy can lower the after-tax cost of acquisition of a property over time by a significant percentage of the purchase price. We term this strategy Enhancement Derivative Planning.

It should be noted, however, that each transaction, every property and the tax status of each taxpayer is unique. Review by knowledgeable persons, attorneys and CPAs is essential. It is critical that your easement team be familiar with easements, land use, tax, law and the real estate market. In addition, it is required that the value of grants be reduced by the amount of value enhancement to reserved rights or adjacent unencumbered land. The concept of value enhancement is simple: Property adjacent to a "park" is more valuable than property adjoining potential development. When one donates an easement on just a part of a rural property, the balance of the land has more value, or is enhanced.

Unsalable Easements

As anecdotal substantiation of the "bad things" that may occur if a Grantor does not reserve rights, consider the case of a several-thousand-acre ranch on the Little Blackfoot River (of *A River Runs Through It* fame), up near Ovando, Montana. It was secluded, end of the road, surrounded by state and other public lands, with miles of the famous river. At the time, with Montana's ranch land boom, this property should have been extremely desirable and completely saleable. I stumbled across the property on an internet search. Several partners and I were in the market at that time for another ranch to improve, operate and enjoy. I was immediately drawn to the land, even on paper. The Blackfoot River Ranch seemed to have it all: river, fishery, prime wildlife habitat, room for value-adding resource improvements, good summer livestock capacity, sixty miles from booming Missoula, privacy and proximity to public lands. I was puzzled that it appeared to be underpriced.

I went up to drive by the property that very day. It was stunning. The aquamarine waters of the Little Blackfoot flowed around serpentine bends in the river. Continual changes in stream structure and visual observation indicated an excellent population of trout. Abundant track, scat and other evidence of whitetail, mule deer and elk herds were everywhere. There was a pristine and secluded feel to it all, a palpable pleasant natural energy. Why had it been on the market for more than six months? Excited, I called the broker when I returned home. I asked him for additional materials. I queried him as to why the property had not sold.

He hemmed and hawed and finally stated, "Some people don't like conservation easements."

"There is a conservation easement on this property?" I asked. He knew full well that under disclosure laws that should have been mentioned upfront.

"Yes, there is," he stammered.

I asked, "And what are the terms of the easement? What rights are reserved?"

"Reserved rights?" the broker responded, evidently puzzled. "What are they?"

I sat at my desk drumming my fingers, heart sinking, and gazed at the brochure's mouth-watering photos, beauty that I had now verified in person.

I replied in a steady voice, "Reserved rights are the rights that the owner reserved when they made the grant of the easement. What could I, if I purchased the ranch, do with this property after purchase? Those are the reserved rights." There was a moment of startled silence.

"I don't think you can subdivide, and I'm not sure if you can build a house on it," he replied.

"Do you mean that somebody allowed this Grantor to give an easement that doesn't allow a single home to be built on a two thousand-plus-acre property? I just spent the day traveling, previewing the property and reviewing basic information. This previously undisclosed conservation easement is a material adverse fact."

The listing agent sensed the incredulity in my voice. The broker stuttered, "I will find out for you. Come to think of it, I may have a copy of the conservation easement somewhere."

I knew what the broker was thinking. This was a property he had not been able to secure a contract on for a long period of time, despite its incredible location and attributes. Now he had a buyer who was well-known in the business, qualified to close, had taken the time to view the ranch, liked it and was obviously interested in submitting an offer. Now here comes this damned conservation easement problem again.

I asked him if he could send me the information and a copy of the easement, along with any baseline resource study. Several days later, I received the information. The advisors to the owners had indeed allowed them to grant an easement with no reserved rights. There was timber on the property that needed to be thinned, which could also generate revenue, increase pasture and forage for livestock and wildlife and reduce fire danger. Timbering, however, was forbidden. Permitted enhancements of the fisheries and wildlife habitat were minimal to nonexistent. The construction of agricultural buildings, including those necessary to simply operate the ranch as a ranch, was forbidden. There were no subdivisions or transfers allowed or reserved. Not a single residential structure, even an owner's house, could be built on the property. A note with the package from the broker indicated one could build a house on an adjoining piece of property that might possibly be purchased from a third party owner. I was extremely disappointed. We did not purchase the ranch. To the best of my knowledge, now, years later, the ranch remains for sale.

Chapter Twenty-Five
Easements in the Current "Class Warfare" Political Environment

I will resist the temptation to get sucked into the whirling vortex of politics. However, politics affects business, land, and decisions.

Will Babies Get Thrown Out with the Bath Water?

There's a definite drumbeat of class warfare in the political currents. Whether or not things are fair, should the "rich" be taxed more? Should the tax code be revised? And if so, how? Do we give folks who need help something to eat, or do we teach them how to fish? And yes, if you've been keeping up on the news, there are tax proposals floating around that would affect charitable giving, probably adversely.

If you follow the press on easements, and I do, there is a difference in the way an easement grant by an "old-time rancher" is treated, and the press related to the grant of an easement on a similar property by a non-generational owner perceived as a "rich guy." In the former case, the grantors are lauded for keeping a way of life, a family and the ranch intact. In the latter case, there is a sometimes not-so-subtle aspersion or insinuation that this is "all about money" assuming the grantor cares far less about the land than they do about the tax benefit. That seems in keeping with the political message of the past few years.

What most folks don't know is that conservation easements typically granted by generational ranches are certainly prompted by the love of land, but in many cases are necessitated by a need for cash. Most of these grants on old-time properties involve more than the donation of property rights—there is a cash payment for a portion of that "donation" to the grantor. Yes, you can *sell* an easement as well as grant one. In Volume Two we will investigate the "easements for cash" phenomena, and as a subheading to that discussion and the real-life stories that go along with it, the grant of non-perpetual easements for finite timeframes, ranging from thirty to sixty years.

The Bush tax cuts contain provisions that enhance the tax benefits flowing from the grant of conservation easements. Prior to the current tax treatment, the grant of an easement resulted in Federal deductions that the grantor could apply (a maximum of 30% per year) to their Adjusted Gross Income (AGI). To the extent the grantor didn't use these federal deductions in any given year, starting with the year in which the easement was granted, they could be carried forward for up to six years.

Under current law, which is set to expire December 31, 2012, and has already been discussed, the tax bennies flowing from the grant of the easement may be applied to up to 50% of your annual AGI, and to the extent not used, will carry forward for 15 years.

One of three things will happen over the next 6 to 12 months:

1) There will be little, if any, change to the current tax-related structure of conservation easement grants; or,

2) Current tax law will expire and the benefits from granting an easement will revert to the 30% per year, maximum six year carry forward, which they had been in the past; or,

3) The rather powerful group known as the Land Trust Alliance, the organization that represents the approximate five thousand land trusts in the United States, and which enjoys fairly widespread bipartisan support, will be able to keep most or all of the benefits that flow from the grant of easements intact.

Better to Have No Easement, than the Wrong Easement

If you've been thinking about an easement, and you get right on it, you may have enough time—between your purchase of this book, and December 31, 2012—to potentially get an easement done on all or a portion of your property, and to take advantage of current tax guidelines. However, rushing an easement (which is perpetual in nature) that can materially affect the real value of your property and your ability to sell in the future—is not a good idea. Far better to have no easement than the wrong easement.

For those of you who are contemplating purchasing, or who own property and have been toying with the idea of the grant of conservation easement, but simply can't marshal your team and forces to get it done prior to December 31, 2012, you are now alerted to the possibility that the benefits that flow from easements may change. It's conceivable, under the worst conditions (given the surreal nature of current politics, and the reality of America's fiscal crisis), that the benefits related to the grant of an easement could be reduced to below what they were in the past. Govern yourself accordingly!

If you are currently working on the grant of a conservation easement, investigating the possibility, or have vaguely contemplated a grant for your land or future land purchase, keep your nose to the wind and your eyes wide open.

Conclusion

This Ain't Your Mama's Sack of Silver

Land—A Class of Its Own

As you know by now, I have a special love and affinity for the land. It is the source of my energy, the precipitator of my passions, the wellspring of my spirit, and both the source and adjunct to my perceptions of personal freedom, self-sufficiency and self-reliance—notions we need to pass onto our children. Hopefully, *Land for Love and Money* gives substance or definition to feelings you may have about the land.

There is nothing quite like land. You can't hunt, fish, farm, or hike on gold and silver. You can't feel energy or grow crops on a stock certificate, or enjoy the view from, or ride a horse on a bond. It's my hope that this first volume of *Land for Love and Money* has provided a good feel for some universal truths about land and afforded useful nuggets about facets of this unique asset that will make or save you money. It is my wish that these books will increase your pleasure on all levels. And, maybe even save you from a few ugly wrecks.

Many of the topics covered here could quite literally be a book unto themselves, and entire books have been written on some of the subjects—not in this style, but detailed and informative. A number are included in the Resources section.

I hope too, that I have introduced the concept of BIG PICTURE THINKING. Engage your brain on a macro basis. You're not buying this asset, owning it, or selling it in a microcosm. Your partnership with your land is a long term commitment! Sure, you have to focus and concentrate on the details of the actual purchase, sale, or management. But understand there are powerful forces at work far larger than your piece of land, your community, your state, and even your country. This "Arc of Influence" will continue to affect land, real estate, you and your family. Sometimes adversely and positively. Being aware of how, and understanding why, can turn the situation to your advantage.

The more people are vested in, know, understand and feel the land, the better stewards they will be. And what's good for the land benefits us all.

A convergence of events can turn the best plans upside down and put your land at risk (look for strategies in Volume Two). In western parlance it is known as "circling the wagons." Harry Potter called it, "Defense against the dark arts." Volume Two contains stories of stormy times, deals gone bad, and the art of defense and offense critical to survival and protection—for you, your land and real estate when everything goes wrong. There will be plenty of positives too, focusing on other aspects of the subjects covered in Volume One, and the "ownership phase"—the management, improvement and enjoyment of land.

Most importantly, I hope I've been able to impart the basic essence, as well as the "hands on" of buying, selling, and owning land. Except in rare cases, you purchase land, enjoy it, and own it because you love it. In most instances you're sorry when you have to sell. But mixed in with love is the money reality. Understanding, integrating, and using this financial reality can make or save you money, and enhance your love affair with your land.

Land—it really is for love and money. *Thank you. Reid.*

Green for Green Workbook Description for Volume One

Each of the volumes of *Land for Love and Money,* including this one, will have an accompanying *Green for Green* workbook in a CD-DVD format. Typically, the workbook will be published 2 to 4 weeks after release of the main volume with which it is associated.

I've worked hard to keep this book engaging and enjoyable. I believe lessons are better learned through stories than textbooks. No one's going to glean significant useful information from a book they simply can't get through. These volumes are meant to provide an overall instructional platform. The workbooks have the nitty-gritty details: forms, charts, and checklists for due diligence, closing, selling and buying, actual excerpts from conservation easements regarding reserved rights and other matters, excerpts from real working documents on deals that are advantageous to the buyer, the seller, or both regarding seller financing, purchase, sale, and protections for the various players involved. Most were developed by me and forged in the fire of thousands of real deals in my career.

The contents of these workbooks have all originated in the crucible of trial and error in the course of more than $1 billion in property business. As an example, the Volume One workbook will contain, just as a sampling:

- Acquisition and Due Diligence Checklists
- Sample contract outline for bare land and improved properties*
- Recommended sales contract provisions*
- Sample real estate commission form
- Sample studies' excerpts on hydrology, soils, mineral, water rights, environmental issues
- Sample maps: resources, enhancements, etc.
- Charts on rural and county governments, departments, and roles of each
- Sample conservation easement and amendment language*
- Sample management agreements (for recreation property, agricultural property, contractors)*

The volumes and the workbooks will also become a series of instructional CDs after both have been published. Updated material, based on current economics, environmental issues, and tax policies will be available on the *Land for Love and Money* website according to its terms, ensuring that *Land for Love and Money* stays relevant in real time, and "evergreen" in this quickly changing political, and mercurial financial landscape.

Though written by attorneys in specific locations for specific transactions, all sample contracts or contract language are provided* ***only* *to afford you a feel and overview of the business concepts—they should* ***not*** *be used until your attorney has reviewed, approved, and or modified the language as your legal representative familiar with local and state laws in your area, and the specifics of your transaction.*

Land for Love and Money: Volumes Two and Three— A Taste

The Land Is Yours: Now What?

In Volume One of *Land for Love and Money,* we talked about writing down what you want in your relationship with the land—what you need, what factors are absolute (your "must have" property attributes), what financial parameters are key to success, and finally, but no less important, connecting with the energy of the land. Whether you purchase a residential home on a one-acre lot, or a five thousand-acre spread, key questions and issues will arise once you've signed the dotted line.

Volumes Two and Three will demonstrate no holds barred truths in the same entertaining, anecdotal, hard-hitting and humorous style as Volume One of *Land for Love and Money.* Volume Two and its following *Green for Green* workbook, will examine additional tips on buyer and seller matters covered in Volume One, the ownership and improvement phase of the land cycle, along with marketing and value adding secrets. Volume Two, given the current economic environment, will also delve into offensive and defensive strategies that work in a crunch; practical advice to guide new and existing owners through a myriad of common, unexpected and sometimes unpleasant situations. Foresight, knowing what to look out for ahead of time, is key to success. PPPPP!

- Of money, management and moxie.
- How am I going to run this place? How can I generate income? Do I need a manager?
- If it ain't broke, why fix it? The "when and how" of making changes and the intricacies of stewardship.
- If it has testicles or tires, it's gonna cause trouble!
- What if I want to fish in my neighbor's pond? The symbiosis of Cross Use Associations©—a unique recreational sharing concept and agreement developed by Reid.
- This damn dog is wagging my tail! Or, what to do when the land starts running *you.*
- Why can't I just wait until tomorrow? Procrastination is *not* your friend.
- Build it and they will come. Creating sanctuary for water fowl, wildlife and livestock.
- You mean there's a federal grant for *that?* Improving the land for everyone.
- I've lived here five years, and they *still* call it the Smith place. Rural, small town conflicts.
- Water wars—"Whiskey is for drinking—water is for fighting." What are my rights?
- What do you mean, they own the mineral rights? Legal trespass and what to do about it.
- Natural disasters—have a plan. Your life and credit depend on it.
- The "land grab" of Eminent Domain—Oh, no you won't, Bubba!
- Defense against the Dark Arts—when a landowner must circle the wagons.

Resources

Agenda 21 (United Nations, Maps and Other Links)

The Local Agenda 21 Planning Guide
http://www.freedomadvocates.org/research_center/

Agenda 21 (United Nations—UN.org): Programme of Action for Sustainable Development, Rio Declaration On Environment and Development, Statement of Forest Principles, © United Nations (Local Agenda Planning Guide)
http://www.freedomadvocates.org/images/pdf/local-agenda-21.pdf

U.N. Department of Economic and Social Affairs Division for Sustainable Development, Agenda 21
http://www.un.org/esa/dsd/agenda21/

U.N. World Heritage and Biosphere Programs in the United States
http://www.un-freezone.org/images/unbiomap2.jpg
http://whc.unesco.org/en/254/ (interactive map)

Appraisals and Appraisers

Appraisal Standards
http://www.treasurer.ca.gov/cdiac/reports/appraisalStds.pdf

Fannie Mae Guidance for Lenders and Appraisers
https://www.efanniemae.com/sf/guides/ssg/relatedsellinginfo/appcode/pdf/appraisalguidance.pdf

Fannie Mae MH Select Appraisal Guidelines
https://www.efanniemae.com/sf/guides/ssg/relatedsellinginfo/manufachousing/pdf/mhselectapprgdlns.pdf

FDIC Interagency Guidance Appraisal and Evaluation Guidelines
http://www.fdic.gov/news/news/financial/2010/fil10082.html

VA Appraisal Fee Schedules and Timeliness Requirements Page (State by State Appraisal Rules)
http://www.benefits.va.gov/homeloans/fee_timeliness.asp

Home Valuation Code of Conduct
https://www.efanniemae.com/sf/guides/ssg/relatedsellinginfo/appcode/pdf/hvcc.pdf

Business/Entities

Limited Liability Company (LLC)
http://www.irs.gov/businesses/small/article/0,,id=98277,00.html

Sub S Corporations
http://www.irs.gov/businesses/small/article/0,,id=98263,00.html

Environmental

Endangered Species Act
http://www.fws.gov/laws/lawsdigest/esact.html

Environmental Quality Incentives Program (EQIP)
http://www.nrcs.usda.gov/wps/portal/nrcs/main/national/programs/financial/eqip

Wildlife Habitat Incentive Program (WHIP)
http://www.nrcs.usda.gov/wps/portal/nrcs/main/national/programs/financial/whip

National Conservation Easement Database (NCED)
http://www.conservationeasement.us/

FDIC

FDIC Law, Regulations, Related Acts
http://www.fdic.gov/regulations/laws/rules/5000-4700.html

FDIC Federal Register Citations
http://www.fdic.gov/regulations/laws/federal/2005/05notice328.html

Federal/State Agencies

Environmental Protection Agency (EPA)
www.epa.gov

Farm Service Agencies (FSA)
http://www.fsa.usda.gov/FSA/webapp?area=home&subject=landing&topic=landing

FarmerMac—Financing Rural America
http://www.farmermac.com/

U.S. Army Corps of Engineers
http://www.usace.army.mil/

U.S. Department of Agriculture (USDA)
http://www.usda.gov/wps/portal/usda/usdahome

U.S. Department of the Interior
http://www.doi.gov/index.cfm

U.S. Department of Housing and Rural Development (HUD)
http://portal.hud.gov/hudportal/HUD

Resolution Trust Corporation
https://www.federalregister.gov/agencies/resolution-trust-corporation

Office of the Comptroller of Currency
http://www.occ.treas.gov/

Financial Statutes/Regulations

Community Reinvestment Act (CRA)
http://ecfr.gpoaccess.gov/cgi/t/text/text-idx?c=ecfr&tpl=/ecfrbrowse/Title12/12cfr25_main_02.tpl

Dodd-Frank Wall Street Reform and Consumer Protection Act Public Law 111 - 203
http://www.gpo.gov/fdsys/pkg/PLAW-111publ203/content-detail.html

Federal Financial Institutions Examination Council
http://www.fdic.gov/regulations/laws/federal/00uniform.pdf

Federal Financial Institutions Examination Council
https://www.ffiec.gov

Financial Institutions Reform, Recovery and Enforcement Act (FIRREA)
http://www.fdic.gov/regulations/laws/rules/8000-3100.html

Truth in Lending Act
http://www.fdic.gov/regulations/laws/rules/6500-1400.html

Homeowners

American Homeowners Association
http://www.ahahome.com

Livestock

Animal Units
http://www.thedairysite.com/articles/981/understanding-the-animal-unit-month-aum

Land Trusts

Land Trust Alliance
http://www.landtrustalliance.org/about

National Community Land Trust Network
http://www.cltnetwork.org

American Farmland Trust
http://www.farmland.org/default.asp

TAX, 1031 and Starker Exchanges

US Tax Code Online
http://www.fourmilab.ch/uscode/26usc/

1031 Exchanges
http://www.1031.org/about1031/faq.htm

1031 Exchanges Made Simple
http://www.1031exchangemadesimple.com

Reverse Starker Exchange
http://www.1031exchangetip.com/reverse-starker-exchange.htm

Glossary

1031 deferred exchange. A 1031 deferred exchange allows a seller to defer tax liabilities on gains of sales of property if strict criteria for investment of the sale proceeds into another like-kind property are met within a specific time period.

Acquirer. A bank that stepped into the shoes of the failed S&L

Agenda 21. The ever evolving bible of globalism, developed by the United Nations in 1992 and purporting to direct and guide countries, their provinces or states and even local municipalities towards environmental sustainability. "Private property ownership is the primary cause of social injustice."

Animal Unit (AU). A standardized measure of animals used for various agricultural purposes, based on a 1,000-pound beef cow as the standard measure.

Animal Unit Month (AUM). The amount of forage needed by an animal unit grazing for one month. Used by land manager to determine stocking rates for range or pasture.

Anti-merger clause. Provisions specified within a Purchase Agreement that provide for warranties that extend forever past closing, without which, such warranties, along with all other prior negotiations and discussions, will merge with closing and be extinguished.

Appraisal. An assessment or estimation of the worth, value, or quality of property for the purpose of assessing tax, determining sales price, or the amount of a mortgage that might be granted on a property.

Articles of Incorporation. The governing document by which the terms and conditions of a Sub-S Corporation are described and made legally binding.

Articles of Organization. The governing document by which the terms and conditions of a Limited Liability Company is described and made legally binding.

Asset. Any valuable item, including cash, stock, inventories, and including property rights.

Bank Examiner. An government auditor who examines, among other things, bank loan files for discrepancies in compliance with banking laws, regulations and rules. Bank examiners visit banks between one and four times a year.

Big brown stonefly nymphs. The subadult stage of the brown stonefly, an aquatic insect which lays eggs, hatches and spends all subadult stages of life in fast moving streams and rivers. A particularly yummy and tantalizing fly imitation used in early spring in the Madison River Watershed for fishing for trout, grayling and whitefish.

Binder. A payment or written statement making an agreement legally binding until the completion of a formal contract, especially an insurance contract.

BM. A euphemism for any partner or member of a Partnership, LP, LLC or S Corp who enters into a Partnership Agreement, and engages in fraudulent activities to the demise of the Partnership, the members and himself.

Buyer's Agency Agreement. A written agreement which sets out the terms and conditions of the relationship between the agent and client, and including such things as the duration of the agreement, the commission to be earned/paid, and the various rights, duties and obligations of the parties.

By Laws. The agreements which set forth and describe the rights, responsibilities, powers, liabilities and authorities of the various shareholders of a S Corporation. Key to the operation of the entity, and it's assets, distribution of profits or benefits, and resolving disputes.

Capital gains. The taxable profit realized on the sale of a long term (12+ months) asset or property.

Capitalization rate (CAP Rate). Annual net operating income/ value. The income from land, when interpolated for valuation as a ratio between the net operating income produced by an asset and its capital cost (the original price paid to buy the asset).

Certificate of Authority. A corporation or limited liability company is domestic to the state in where it was formed. Land ownership via an LLC, LP or S-Corps outside the state in which it is domiciled might require a Certificate of Authority, without which, the partnership may be subject to fines and legal action by the state in which it would be illegally transacting business. If a Certificate of Authority is filed, the partnership is subject to taxes and fees in both the state of formation and any states where the partnership is qualified.

Comparables. Also referred to as Comps are properties similar to the property being appraised, located in the immediate or like market areas.

Conforming property. A term defined by the financing industry to describe property that meets certain requirements in order to qualify for mortgage financing.

Deed of Trust. A written agreement legally conveying property to a trustee, often used to secure an obligation such as a promissory note.

Dodd–Frank Wall Street Reform and Consumer Protection Act (Dodd-Frank). (Pub.L. 111-203, H.R. 4173) A federal statute, signed into law by President Barack Obama on July 21, 2010. A bureaucratic knee-jerk reaction to the great meltdown of 2008, it affects all federal financial regulatory agencies and almost every aspect of the nation's financial services industry.

Dwelling Unit (DU). Where zoning or other government overlayment might allow typical lot or small acreage subdivision (three and one-half houses per acre—aka 3.5/ D.U.)

Due diligence. An investigation, normally by the buyer, of a potential target for acquisition focusing on existing conditions and material future matters.

Eminent domain. An action of the government to seize a citizen's private property, expropriate property, or seize a citizen's rights in property, without the owner's consent, either for use or by delegation to third parties who will devote it to public or civic use or, in some cases, economic development. Some monetary compensation is provided. The most common uses of property taken by eminent domain are for public utilities, highways, and railroads.

Enhancement Derivative Planning. A term referring to planning strategy in which resource, agricultural, and other improvements to the property, result in real increases in value which may lead to very significant escalation of tax benefits. The grant of easements can also increase the value of adjacent lands not subject to easement, and of the rights that have been reserved. Depending upon the individual Grantor's tax status, this strategy can lower the after-tax cost of acquisition of a property over time by a significant percentage of the purchase price.

Farm Service Agency (FSA). The federal agency tasked with the implementation of farm conservation and regulation laws around the country.

Farmer Mac—Federal Agricultural Mortgage Corporation. A stockholder-owned, government sponsored enterprise, created by Congress in 1988 to provide a secondary market in agricultural loans, and the guaranteed portions of agricultural and rural development loans guaranteed by the United States Department of Agriculture. Farmer Mac purchases loans from agricultural lenders, and sells instruments backed by those loans, Farmer Mac is responsible for guaranteeing the repayment of principal and interest to investors.

Federal Deposit Insurance Corporation (FDIC). A government corporation which examines and supervises certain financial institutions, provides deposit insurance which guarantees the safety of deposits in member banks (up to $250,000 per depositor per bank as of January 2012), and manages Acquirers and failed banks via a Loss Share Agreement.

Fence-out laws. In certain states, landowners are required to build and maintain fences to keep *out* livestock.

Financial Institutions Reform, Recovery, and Enforcement Act of 1989 (FIRREA). Enacted in the wake of the Savings And Loan crisis of the 1980s, it established the Resolution Trust Corporation as successor to the FSLIC to close hundreds of insolvent thrifts and provided funds to pay out insurance to their depositors.

For Sale by Owner (FSBO). The process of selling real estate without the representation of a real estate broker or real estate agent.

Foreclosure. The process by which a lender attempts to recover the balance of a loan from an asset; a forced borrower sale of the asset used as the collateral for the loan.

FSLIC (Federal Savings and Loan Insurance Corporation). The quasi-government entity that was responsible for insuring deposits in Savings and Loan institutions until the savings and loan crisis of the 1980s, at which time it became insolvent; and was abolished by the FIRREA in 1989, and the deposit insurance responsibility was transferred to the FDIC as manager of the FRF (FSLIC Resolution Fund) as manager of the RTC.

General Partnerships. A basic business partnership, formed by two or more partners and created by Agreement, or an Partnership Agreement. The members, called Partners, share equally, and are all personally liable for any legal actions and debts the company may face. There is no managing partner. General Partnerships may or may not have a written Agreement.

Grantor. The person donating or selling an easement, or instrument of conveyance.

Homeowners association. A corporation formed for the purpose of marketing, managing, and maintaining properties in a residential subdivision.

Joint Venture. A business partnership in which parties agree to develop a new entity and new assets by contributing equity. The members or partners share revenues, expenses and assets. Similar to a General Partnership.

Like-kind exchange. A transaction that allows for the disposition of property and the acquisition of another, "like" property without generating a tax liability from the sale of the first.

Limited Liability Company (LLC). A partnership in which the owners, or members, are protected from some or all liability of the LLC, registered under Articles of Organization. LLCs are run by manager(s), and governed via rights, responsibilities, powers, liabilities and authorities as described in an Operating Agreement.

Limited Partner. The partner in a Limited Partnership.

Limited Partnership (LP). A partnership in which the owners are called limited partners. Only one partner is required to be a General Partner (many times a corporate entity). Registered with the state under a Partnership Registration the agreements which govern the rights, responsibilities, powers, liabilities and authorities key to the operation of the entity, and it's assets, distribution of profits or resolving disputes is Limited Partnership Agreement.

Loan to value ratio (LTV). The ratio of the loan amount to equity based on appraisal. Example: If your appraisal is $100, and the loan is $50, you have a 50% LTV.

Long-term capital gains. A profit or value of property accrued over an extended period time greater than one year.

Loss Share Agreement. A agreement made between the FDIC and lenders, under which the acquiring banks are encouraged to purchase loans of failed banks at a significant discount, but are guaranteed profits, funded by the taxpayers by the FDIC on the face amount of those loans.

Macroeconomics. Conceptual reference to economics dealing with the performance, structure, behavior, and governmental decision-making of the whole economy, including national, regional, and global economies including government policy, taxation and regulation.

MAI. A professional designation held by appraisers who are experienced in the valuation and evaluation of commercial, industrial, residential and other types of properties, and who advise clients on real estate investment decisions.

Managers. The member(s) of a LLC that carries management authority.

Material affects. Either positive or negative, significant affects to property value and salability from environmental impacts, development and encumbrances.

Member. The partner in a Limited Liability Company.

Metaphysical. Referring to that which is without material form or substance; not existing in nature or subject to explanation according to natural laws; neither physical nor material.

Millage tax. See property tax.

Nonperforming asset. A classification level by which a loan no longer qualifies for continued financing, including loans on which payments of interest and principal are not being made.

Northern Laramie Range Alliance (NLRA). An association of citizens and dedicated to preserving the open-space, agricultural and recreational character of the Northern Laramie Mountains in central Wyoming. Formed in March 2009 when it became evident that the Northern Laramies have been targeted for industrial-scale wind energy development.

Office of the Comptroller of Currency (OCC). An independent bureau within the U.S. Department of Treasury, established by the National Currency Act of 1863 and serves to charter, regulate, and supervise all national banks, and the federal branches and agencies of foreign banks in the United States.

Operating Agreement. A legally binding document which governs the rights, responsibilities, powers, liabilities and authorities of the various partners of an LLC, and key to the operation of the entity, management of its assets, distribution of profits or other benefits, or resolving disputes.

Partnership Agreement. The written agreement by which the terms and conditions of a partnership are described and made legally binding.

Performing. A term used to describe a loan for which payments of principle and interest are consistent with the terms set forth in the loan agreement. Also a level of classification used by bank examiners to rate loan files.

Phantom income. Taxable income based taxable gain or proportionate shares of taxable gain of an S-Corp, LLC, or LP, in excess of cash distributions regardless.

PPPPP Rule. "Prior planning prevents poor performance."

Property tax or millage tax. A tax levied on property including: land, improvements to land, personal property, and intangible property, by the governing authority of the jurisdiction in which the property is located.

PTO or Power take-off. That point at which implements may be attached to machinery and from which power is transferred from the machinery, to a drive shaft and gear box attachment on the implement.

Reserved rights. Property rights reserved by the owner, and therefore not donated, sold or otherwise transferred as conditions of a conservation easement.

Review appraisal or second appraisal. An appraisal done to provide valuation on a property should the lender determine that the property require more scrutiny, is unique, or if comparable properties are difficult to obtain or not available.

Riparian area protection fence. A fence designed and constructed to manage access to riparian zones with the purpose of restoration and protection of habitat within the riparian corridor and streambed.

S&L—Savings and loan association. Also known as a thrift, is a financial institution that specializes in accepting savings deposits and making mortgage and other loans.

Seller financing. A loan provided by the seller of a property to the buyer, rather than the buyer obtaining financing from a bank.

Shareholder. The partner in a Sub-S Corporation.

SRA. A professional designation held by appraisers who are experienced in the analysis and valuation of residential real property.

Starker Exchange. Exchange of certain types of property to defer the recognition of capital gains or losses due upon sale, and hence defer any capital gains taxes otherwise due.

Sub S Corporation (S-Corp). A specialized corporation in which the members or shareholders share liabilities, profits and losses.

Terms. Conditions and provisions of a purchase agreement, softer terms typically mean more lenient provisions, and a higher price. Stiff terms such as an all-cash deal, typically mean a price discount.

Thrift. A savings and loan association, credit union, or savings bank.

Title Insurance Commitment. A commitment by a qualified surety, to insure merchantable title to a properly.

Triple mocha. An overpriced coffee beverage usually containing three (hence the name) shots of chocolate syrup and three shots of espresso.

U.S. Tax Code. The approximately eighty thousand pages of the domestic portion of Federal statutory tax law covering income tax, payroll taxes, estate taxes, gift taxes and excise taxes; as well as procedure and administration.